More Praise for *Twins 101*

"When I found I was having twins, I searched for books that would be able to give me research- and experiential-based information, and there was nothing out there until *Twins 101*."

—*Eileen Andrade Kitching, M.S., C.C.L.S., child life director, University of California, Irvine; mother of twins*

"*Twins 101* is filled with practical advice and insights that will be welcome reading for all parents expecting or raising twins."

—*Henry Lee, M.D., neonatologist, Stanford University*

"This book contains high-yield, easy-to-read tips, making it convenient for busy, on-the-go parents of multiples. Dr. Le-Bucklin demystifies the NICU and familiarizes readers with medical jargon that can be overwhelming to new parents. Nobody could have been better qualified to write this book than Dr. Le-Bucklin as a pediatrician and an amazing M.O.M."

—*Henry J. Legere III, M.D., Brigham and Women's Hospital, Boston; pediatrician and author,* Raising Healthy Eaters: 100 Tips for Parents

"This is a fantastic reference for any parent who has twins or multiples. This book provides exceptional insight for parents of twins that can relieve stress and anxiety in a fast-paced life."

—*Eric D. Schultz, D.O., M.P.H., pediatrician, Duke University Medical Center*

Twins 101

50 Must-Have Tips
for Pregnancy Through
Early Childhood
from Doctor M.O.M.

Khanh-Van Le-Bucklin, M.D., M.O.M.*

*Mother of Multiples

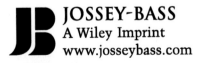
JOSSEY-BASS
A Wiley Imprint
www.josseybass.com

Published by Jossey-Bass
A Wiley Imprint
989 Market Street, San Francisco, CA 94103-1741—www.josseybass.com

Readers should be aware that Internet Web sites offered as citations and/or sources for further information
may have changed or disappeared between the time this was written and when it is read.

Limit of Liability/Disclaimer of Warranty: While the publisher and author have used their best
efforts in preparing this book, they make no representations or warranties with respect to the accuracy
or completeness of the contents of this book and specifically disclaim any implied warranties of
merchantability or fitness for a particular purpose. No warranty may be created or extended by sales
representatives or written sales materials. The advice and strategies contained herein may not be suitable
for your situation. You should consult with a professional where appropriate. Neither the publisher nor
author shall be liable for any loss of profit or any other commercial damages, including but not limited to
special, incidental, consequential, or other damages.

The anecdotes in this book are based on the clinical experience and research of the author. To protect
confidentiality, some of the names and identifying characteristics have been changed or represent
composite identities.

Jossey-Bass books and products are available through most bookstores. To contact Jossey-Bass
directly call our Customer Care Department within the U.S. at 800-956-7739, outside the U.S. at
317-572-3986, or fax 317-572-4002.

Jossey-Bass also publishes its books in a variety of electronic formats. Some content that appears
in print may not be available in electronic books.

Library of Congress Cataloging-in-Publication Data
Le-Bucklin, Khanh-Van.
  Twins 101 : 50 must-have tips for pregnancy through early childhood from doctor m.o.m. /
Khanh-Van Le-Bucklin. — 1st ed.
    p. cm.
  Includes bibliographical references and index.
  ISBN 978-0-470-34368-5 (pbk.)
  1. Twins. 2. Multiple pregnancy—Popular works. 3. Multiple birth—Popular works.
4. Infants—Care. 5. Parenting. I. Title.
  HQ777.35.L43   2009
  649'.144—dc22   2008022739

FIRST EDITION
PB Printing   10 9 8 7 6 5 4 3 2

CONTENTS

*To all the mothers who have guided me on my parenting journey
and to all the mothers of twins to come.
May this book connect us as parents of multiples.
May the priceless wisdom of veteran mothers find its way
to blessed new mothers through this book.*

ACKNOWLEDGMENTS

Writing this book has been much like raising twins: at once challenging and thrilling. In the end, you know you have achieved something unique and wonderful. And you realize that you could not have accomplished any of it without the help of so many generous supporters along the way.

First, I thank all the mothers who have so kindly and graciously guided me through my ongoing journey as a mother of twins. I could not have written this book without their insight and wisdom.

My deep appreciation to Alan Rinzler, executive editor at Jossey-Bass, for being such an amazing literary mentor and believing in me as a writer. Alan, I am honored to have had the opportunity to work with you! Thank you to publisher, Paul Foster, for his support of this book. Thank you to all the staff at Jossey-Bass who helped with the editing, production, and marketing of this book, including Nana Twumasi, Beverly Miller, Carol Hartland, Jennifer Wenzel, Jeff Puda, Beverly Butterfield, Paula Goldstein, Sophia Ho, Michael Onorato, and Susan Geraghty. Thanks to Shii McDuff for taking photographs for the book.

Special thanks to Kimberly Douglas, Angela Sun, and Anh Tran for their insightful quotes and tips. Thanks to Alan Greene, Cheryl Greene, and Elise Proulx for paving the way for me to write this book.

ACKNOWLEDGMENTS

I want to acknowledge the chair of my department at the University of California, Irvine, Feizal Waffarn, for his support, especially during my pregnancy. Thank you to Donna Peach, Margaret Zimmerman, Brinda Singh, Carla Busto, Carolyn Moser, Jodi Richardson, Kirat Malhi, and Jennifer Lai for keeping the residency running smoothly during my pregnancy and thereafter.

Thank you to Bich-Van Tran, Manuel Porto, Deborah Wing, Jack Sills, and Cherry Uy for providing exceptional medical care to me and my twin daughters, Faith and Hope. Thank you to all the nurses and other great doctors at the University of California, Irvine Medical Center who forever touched our lives with their kindness and brilliant clinical expertise.

I am deeply grateful to all our relatives and friends for their support, prayers, cooked meals, and free babysitting. Special thanks to my siblings and their spouses—Anh-Tuan Le, Linhsan Le, Jessica Le, Luke Dalfiume, Anne Le, Hong-Van Le, Jason Tuffs, Tasha Le, and Gustavo Delgado—for being like second parents to our children.

Thank you to Langdon and Rose Bucklin for their love, humor, and support. Thank you to my father, Tung Van Le, for giving me a passion for science and for always encouraging me to pursue my dreams. My wholehearted appreciation to my mother, Ngoc-Dieu Nguyen, for her steadfast love and immeasurable generosity in caring for me and my children.

A heartfelt thanks to my dear husband, Chris, who has been not only the love of my life but also a true friend and wonderful partner in parenthood. To my lovely children Hannah, Faith, and

Hope, thank you for your never-ending smiles, hugs, and patience. You are the most amazing children, and I thank God every day for you.

Faith and Hope, your mere existence is a miracle. You are such survivors! You remind me that anything is possible with faith and hope. I love being a mother to you, and I am truly "doubly blessed" by you. Thank you for being the inspiration for this book.

Khanh-Van Le-Bucklin
October 2008

INTRODUCTION

On a sunny February afternoon in Orange County, California, I decide to entrust my children, a pair of seven-month-old twin girls and their three-year-old sister, to their father while I take a break—a short drive to the local department store on a quest to replenish our dwindling supply of baby wipes and diapers.

A couple of spots down from where I park, a petite blonde woman merrily pushes a double-stroller up to her black Suburban SUV. Two adorable boys dressed alike in orange T-shirts chat with each other while sitting tandem in their double-stroller. I surmised that they were about three years old. And no doubt about it, they were . . . twins!

Intrigued, I watch as the woman purposefully parks the stroller alongside the car and steps on the stroller brakes—true signs of an experienced mother of twins. I remember the time I parked my twins in their stroller in back of the car and took one girl out—then saw with horror that the stroller started sliding backward toward the street. Did I move fast!

This veteran mother quickly transfers one twin out of the stroller and into the car while managing to keep a watchful eye on the other. She hands one boy a toy to keep him occupied while she lifts his brother into the car. Closing the second-row passenger door, she then proceeds to begin loading the huge stroller and some shopping bags into the trunk of her car.

As I marvel at the efficiency and fluidity with which she cares for her children, I walk by and say, "Your children are adorable! I have three children, and two are twins."

Her face lights up. "Twins! What a trip!" Instantly the other mother of twins and I bond over our experience as parents of multiples. "How old are they?"

"Seven months," I reply. "I can't wait until they are your children's age. You handle them so gracefully!"

"Thank you!" She smiles. Encouragingly she continues, "I've had a lot of practice. When they are young, it can be really tough, but it does get a lot easier."

"I hope so!" I exclaim. "They are so much fun, but they are so much work!"

"I know!" she says. "What kept me sane was keeping them on a schedule. It's really important to keep them on a schedule."

"I'm so glad you said that!" I sigh in relief. "You hear so much these days that we're supposed to let our babies make their own schedules, and that may be okay for one kid at a time, but it doesn't work for me. I couldn't get any rest or sleep with infant twins on random schedules."

"Absolutely!" she says. "It's not the same with twins. My boys are three, and I still have them on a schedule!"

I listen eagerly as she graciously offers more advice while packing up her car.

"When they get older, try making an entire room where they can hang out safely by themselves. When our boys started to crawl, we took all the furniture out of the living room and made it a big playroom. Then we didn't have to go crazy trying to keep them out of trouble.

"And make sure you have time to yourself. I'm glad to see you are out by yourself right now. I went batty until I realized that I needed time to myself to reenergize."

Just then the two cute boys poke their heads out from behind the back seat and holler in synchrony, "Mom! We're hungry!"

"I better let you go," I say. "Thank you so much for all your great advice!"

Liberated by her last tip, I decide to enter the department store and shop guilt free. Not half an hour into my shopping trip, a very pregnant woman in a motorized shopping cart nearly runs me over in the infant clothing section.

"Oops," she says. "I'm so sorry. I'm really not used to this contraption. My doctor says I have to use it to keep the twins from being born too early."

"Congratulations! I have twins at home. What a coincidence!" I exclaim. An immediate connection forms as we laugh over how many people we nearly injured driving the motorized shopping cart around tight corners.

As we talk, she hesitantly inquires, "How are your twins? Are they okay now?"

I see her sweep her hands protectively over her abdomen, and I say, "My twins are doing great! They were born premature and had some problems in the beginning, but they're seven months old now and doing fantastic."

"That's so great to hear!" she says. "I've been really worried about this pregnancy.

"Do you like being a mother to twins? Is it doable?"

"Definitely!" I answer. "It's so much work from pregnancy onward, but every bit of it is worth it. You're going to love being a mother to twins."

"I'm really excited," she responds, "but I'm so nervous. I have a teenage daughter, and I haven't cared for a baby in years. And now, two of them at once! Oh my gosh."

"You'll do great." I try to reassure her, touching her lightly on the arm. "Every twin mother I've spoken to has said that she was surprised and proud of her ability to step up to the challenge. The fact that you care this much is a great sign of how wonderful a mother you're going to be to your twins.

"How many more weeks do you have to go?"

"Another month or so," she says, looking pretty exhausted. "It's really hard to be on bed rest for this long."

"I know!" I reply. "I remember how hard it was to literally lie in wait for the due date to come."

Having recently been in the same situation, I share some advice and words of encouragement. "One thing that kept me motivated was remembering how good it was for my babies for me to rest. When you're not up and about, lie down on your side as much as possible to increase blood flow to the babies. For moral support, you can perform a Web search to find and then join online community discussions with other mothers on bed rest. Bed rest can sometimes be difficult, but shopping with a motorized cart like this is a great way to get out while sticking to your doctor's prescription to stay off your feet. Believe me, you are much more talented on that cart than I ever was!"

She laughs and thanks me for my advice. "Thanks so much for talking with me!" she says appreciatively. "I feel so much better knowing someone has been through the same thing and every-thing worked out well for her in the end."

Why I Wrote This Book

An unspoken sisterhood exists between mothers of multiples. The instant they meet, they are bonded by a shared understanding of the joys and challenges of parenting multiples. They want to encourage each other. They freely admit their mistakes as they relate their experience for the sake of the other mother. Novice mothers attentively seek advice while more veteran mothers graciously impart it. This spirit of sisterhood and sharing provided the inspiration for writing this book.

My personal journey with twins began with two unusually solid blue lines on a pregnancy test strip. Two stripes, you're pregnant. One stripe, you're not. I knew the routine from my prior pregnancy with my then two-year-old daughter.

What made this test different was an unusual clarity to the blue stripes considering that the test was done at least a week before my period would have arrived. I remember with my first daughter that we could barely tell if there was a second line. But with this test, the two blue lines emerged quickly and solidly, indicating that my pregnancy hormone level was surging. In retrospect, my hormone level was unusually high because I was pregnant with twins.

Seven weeks into my pregnancy, I started spotting. An ultrasound to evaluate the bleeding surprised both me and my obstetrician when two little bodies appeared on the screen. I couldn't believe I was pregnant with twins!

As the weeks passed, I continued to have regular ultrasounds to monitor the health of the twins. With amazement, I saw the babies transform from two tiny white masses on the screen into two fully formed babies. There were many challenges along the way, but before I knew it, I was on the laboring table giving birth. What started out as two beautiful blue stripes on a pregnancy test culminated in the birth of two beautiful girls, Faith and Hope. Parenting them has been a learning and rewarding experience.

From the day I found out I was pregnant with twins, I knew I was embarking on a special journey. Mothers of multiples openly share what they have learned from their experiences because they understand that parenting twins can be very different from rearing singletons. I am writing this book to guide others on the unique and fantastic adventure of raising twins.

Although this book specifically addresses twins, many of the tips also apply to parenting triplets and other high-order multiples. I hope these tips provide a source of help and inspiration to parents and other fortunate caregivers of twin babies.

How This Book Works

Parents of twins are busy people. We don't have any spare time to sit down and read a book from beginning to end like a novel or history book, so I designed this book to suit the active lifestyle of a parent of multiples.

Instead of long, time-consuming chapters, I have organized the book into fifty brief, easy-to-read tips plus boxed sections containing twin facts, innovative hints, and insightful stories. This book provides a wealth of information in increments that accommodate your schedule. Busy parents of twins can easily read one tip at a time during the brief pauses in their day. In the middle of the night when you need answers, you can refer to this book for quick ideas and solutions.

The first fifteen tips offer instruction for maintaining a healthy twin pregnancy. During pregnancy, the care required for twins differs from that of a single baby. Specialists and tests that one may never consider in a normal single pregnancy become crucial in a twin pregnancy. Women pregnant with twins can also maximize the health of their babies by eating appropriately, bonding with their unborn babies, and learning how to cope with the unique challenges of a twin pregnancy.

The date of delivery is the day every mother looks forward to, and a twin pregnancy requires preparing for that day far in advance. Tips 16 to 20 address the key questions mothers with multiples have about their anticipated delivery. How do I know I am in labor? Can I deliver vaginally? Where will I deliver? Who will be there when I deliver? This information prepares mothers for the experience of birthing multiples while providing ideas for how to make the experience pleasurable and memorable.

For most families, the homecoming immediately follows the delivery of twins. However, some baby twins may be born premature and require time to grow in the hospital prior to coming home. A special hospital ward, the Neonatal Intensive Care Unit (NICU), provides a temporary home for these babies. Tips 21 to 26 address families whose babies require care in the NICU.

At last, the babies are ready to come home, and caring parents want to buy everything they can to make both parents and babies comfortable. It's very easy to waste an enormous amount of money on this pursuit. Tips 27 to 31 provide practical advice on how to avoid shopping pitfalls and to save money while meeting the needs of twins.

Raising twins means double the work—and double the blessings. At first, the work seems more challenging than anyone could ever imagine. However, in Tips 32 to 50, you will find easy, parent-tested ways to simplify your child care duties. From feeding to dressing to sleep-training twins, Tips 32 to 50 offer ideas for making these daily activities fun and easier to do.

What Is My Background

The collection of fifty tips in this book is a result of experience gained through my two degrees, my M.D. (doctor of medicine degree) and my M.O.M. (Mother of Multiples degree).

As a physician, I am no stranger to giving advice on the care of twins, so many of the tips provided in this book originate from my medical training in pediatrics. I earned my medical degree in 1998 from the University of California, San Francisco. Following medical school, I completed my pediatric residency training at Stanford University. It was at Stanford where I first provided medical care to twins and high-order multiples. I have enjoyed caring for multiples ever since.

My career has been devoted to teaching others how to care for children. I have over fifteen years of experience in health education. Currently I direct multiple aspects of patient and physician education at the University of California, Irvine (UCI). I oversee the education of medical students, future pediatricians, and other health care providers through my roles as pediatric electives director, pediatric residency program director, and pediatric continuing medical education director.

In addition to teaching health care providers, I enjoy interacting personally with parents and promoting child health through my job as a faculty pediatrician at UCI. I also have over eight years of experience as the senior medical content editor for a popular pediatric Web site, DrGreene.com. In this role, I help deliver parenting advice to a massive number of families nationwide.

When I became pregnant with twins, I wanted to read everything I could on twins. Not surprisingly, I found that the majority of information I needed was not on standard bookstore shelves but in medical books and journals.

As a physician, I was thankful for the access I had to these medical resources. However, I quickly realized that what parents of twins really need is a book for them—a book that has all the information available to researchers and clinicians but in a form that parents can quickly read and easily grasp. For this book, I have used my medical background and personal experience to translate current research and medical knowledge into useful information for parents of twins.

Although my medical degree certainly helped me to write this book, being a mother of twins is the most important way I have learned to appreciate the many trials and joys of parenting twins. I discovered some of the tips I share in this book through troubleshooting challenges on my own. Other tips are derived from the collective wisdom of veteran mothers before me. Every mother of twins deserves a special degree. In the world of multiples, this degree is called the M.O.M. degree. I earned mine from the "University of Caring for Faith and Hope." Without this degree, I could not have written this book.

As a physician, a common question I receive from parents is, "What would you do if you were in my shoes?" When it comes to twins, I can enthusiastically answer, "This is what I would do, not only because I am a doctor but because I *have* been in your shoes."

CHAPTER 1

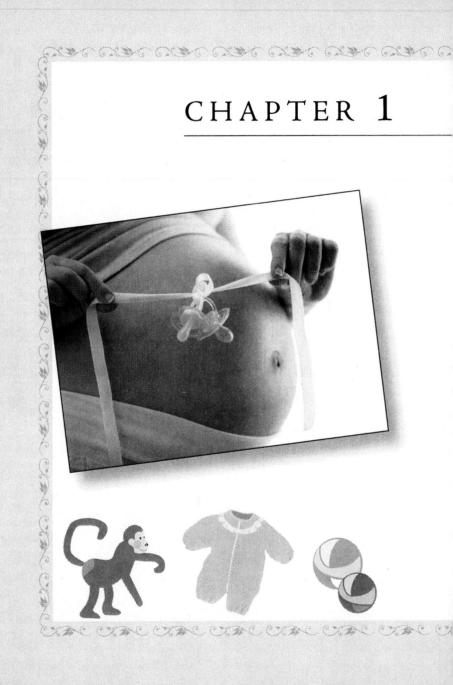

Pregnancy

TIP #1: Congratulate Yourself and Celebrate!

My eyes stared at the black-and-white image on the screen. Seven weeks pregnant and spotting, I held my breath as my obstetrician performed a fetal ultrasound to look for signs of life. I knew the statistics: if she found a heartbeat, the chances of survival for the baby would be over 90 percent.

As the ultrasound probe scanned my uterus, a flickering heart popped up on the screen. "Congratulations!" she said. "You are definitely pregnant, and it looks like the baby is doing fine." Tears welled in my eyes as I looked at my healthy baby.

Just then we saw a whitish mass. "This could be a little blood clot," she said. Just as soon as she said that, we both gasped. Indeed, the mass was not a clot at all! There on the screen was a flickering heart—another flickering heart. Two hearts. Two babies. Twins!

"The moment." Every mother of twins has it. It is the instant when you discover that you are pregnant with twins. You find yourself momentarily speechless. You feel shocked by the news, joyful that you are going to have twins, and fearful of the unknown. You will never forget this life-changing event.

If you have just recently learned that you are expecting twins, I want to be one of the first to welcome you to the world of multiples! You have every reason to be proud and to congratulate yourself. Every year, approximately one in sixty birthing mothers find themselves blessed with twins, and you will soon be one of them.

A wonderful journey lies ahead. Having twins means hard work during pregnancy and after. But the rewards outweigh the

TWIN FACTS *What's in a Name?*

The word *twin* comes from the Old English word
getwinn, which means "twin," "two by two," or "double."

investment. You will experience not only double the work but also
double the joy. Imagine twice the number of hugs and kisses, twice
the smiles and laughter!

You can look forward to twin memories that only parents of
multiples have the opportunity to experience: the first time your
twins smile at each other, the first time they talk to one another,
the first time both babies plant you with a kiss. These precious
moments await you.

When I found out I was pregnant with twins, I was so
thrilled and excited, I couldn't stop shaking for days. At the same
time, part of me was shaking because I had no idea what future lay
ahead. I'm writing this book to tell you that a wonderful journey
awaits you. Congratulate yourself and celebrate!

T I P #2: Remember You Are Not Alone

My hands quivered as I dialed the number to my husband's office.
Since we already had one child, I had discouraged my spouse
from coming to the obstetrician with me, thinking this would be a
routine visit. When he picked up the phone, I blurted out, "There
are two!"

"Two of what?" he asked.

"Babies. There are two babies!"

TWIN FACTS *Twins Go Hollywood*

Consider yourself a star! Twins seem to be en vogue among celebrities these days. On November 28, 2004, actress Julia Roberts kicked off a new celebrity trend with the birth of boy-girl twins, Phinnaeus Walter and Hazel Patricia. Now check out this list of recent celebrity parents of twins:

- Joan Lunden (broadcaster) and Jeff Konigsberg; parents to boy-girl twins, Jack Andrew and Kimberly Elise, born March 1, 2005. This is Lunden's second set of twins. Her first set, boy-girl twins Max and Kate, were born June 10, 2003.
- Melissa Etheridge (singer-songwriter) and Tammy Lynn Michaels (actress); parents to boy-girl twins, Miller Steven and Johnnie Rose, born October 17, 2006.
- Elvis Costello (singer-songwriter) and Diana Krall (singer); parents to twin boys, Dexter Henry Lorcan and Frank Harlan James, born December 6, 2006.
- Sean "P. Diddy" Combs (record producer, actor, rapper) and Kimberly Porter; parents to twin girls, D'Lila Star and Jessie James, born December 21, 2006.
- Patrick Dempsey (actor) and Jillian Fink Dempsey; parents to twin boys, Darby Galen and Sullivan Patrick, born February 1, 2007.
- Marcia Cross (actress) and Tom Mahoney; parents to twin girls, Eden and Savannah, born February 20, 2007.

- Mia Hamm (soccer player) and Nomar Garciaparra (baseball player); parents to twin girls, Grace Isabella and Ava Caroline, born March 28, 2007.
- Garcelle Beauvais-Nilon (actress) and Mike Nilon; parents to twin boys, Jax Joseph and Jaid Thomas, born October 18, 2007.
- Nancy Grace (talk show host) and David Linch; parents to boy-girl twins, John David and Lucy Elizabeth, born November 4, 2007.
- Dennis Quaid (actor) and Kimberly Quaid; parents to boy-girl twins, Thomas Boone and Zoe Grace, born November 8, 2007.
- Jennifer Lopez (actress, singer-songwriter) and Marc Anthony (singer); parents to boy-girl twins, Max and Emme, born February 22, 2008.

Dazed, he asked, "You mean we're having twins?"

The image of the two hearts flashed before me. Two tiny bodies sharing one placenta. "Yes, twins," I said trembling. "Identical twins."

Twin shock—a commonly used term in the world of multiples to describe the body-numbing, speechless state of bewilderment that accompanies the news or reality of having twins. If you are like me, twin shock can hit the moment you find out you are pregnant with twins. For others, twin shock most powerfully strikes shortly after the birth of twins, when parents assume full care of two active newborn babies. Regardless of when twin shock hits, it's a completely normal phase in parenting multiples.

TWIN FACTS *Your Chances of Having Twins*

So what are your chances of having twins?

+ Three percent, or one out of every thirty-three births, for women under thirty-five years of age.
+ About 6 percent, or one in eighteen births, for women over thirty-five years old.
+ Twenty percent, or one in five births, for women forty-five to forty-nine years of age.
+ For women ages fifty to fifty-four, one of every two births will be a multiple delivery. In other words, these women have a 50 percent chance of having twins, triplets, or more!

Most families at this stage are ecstatic about having twins. At the same time, they may have some questions about raising two babies at once. You may have fears or concerns about your pregnancy and potential complications. You may wonder how you are going to physically or financially care for twins.

You are not alone! In fact, you are among a rapidly growing population of parents. The number of twin births in the United States is at an all-time high. Twins now comprise one in thirty-one births, totaling more than 130,000 births a year. Nationally, the number of twin births has increased by 70 percent over the past two decades, and the number of triplets and higher has increased by an astounding 300 percent! What is more, this remarkable upward trend in multiple births is expected to continue.

One major reason for the increase in twin births is that women are having children later than they used to. Older women are more likely to have twins when they become pregnant because they naturally are prone to releasing more than one egg each month. Older women are also more likely to use fertility-enhancing treatments, the single most influential factor in increasing the twinning rate over the past two decades.

One of the most rewarding things about being a parent to twins is the camaraderie among twin families. I recommend that every parent of multiples seek out a few other families of multiples for friendship and support as soon as possible. Time with other twin parents allows you to share in the joy of parenting twins, gives you a sense of pride in your achievements, and offers you priceless advice when you most need it.

TWIN FACTS *Got Yams?*

Nigeria boasts the world's highest spontaneous twinning rate, at about one in twenty-two births. The secret behind this high multiple birth rate may lie partly in yams, a staple of the rural Nigerian diet. Experts theorize that yams, which contain natural hormone-like substances, may increase the chances of a twin conception by stimulating a woman's ovaries to release more than one egg at a time.

TWIN FACTS *Oldest Twin Mother*

The oldest woman to give birth to surviving twins is from Spain. In 2006, the unidentified Spanish mother gave birth to twins at sixty-seven years of age!

If you don't know anyone with twins, contact your local mothers of multiples chapter or the National Organization of Mothers of Twins Clubs. The National Organization of Mothers of Twins Clubs has over twenty-five thousand members and over 450 local clubs. If there are no twin families nearby, there are great online communities that you can join. Some are listed in the Resources section at the end of this book.

Entering into the world of multiples is like joining a band of sisters. Mothers of multiples care about each other and want others to succeed. They openly provide support, wisdom, understanding, and advice to each other. You are in for a wonderful journey, and there are many sisters who will join you on your way. You're in great company!

TWIN FACTS *Twins Marrying Other Twins*

If a set of identical twins marries another set of identical twins, their children will be full siblings genetically, even though legally, they are cousins.

TIP #3: Don't Worry About All the Horror Stories

During my pregnancy with twins, I heard many tragic stories of twin miscarriages, twins who died after birth, and twins who suffered severe disabilities.

The problem with many of these stories was the lack of details. It's easy to become overly worried if you focus on all the horror stories and then apply them to your own situation without knowing the details.

Parents of multiples may also worry when they read certain twin statistics in books, articles, or Internet resources. Certainly

---

TWIN FACTS *Smallest Surviving Twin Babies*

Rumaisa Rahman, a twin, holds the record for being the smallest surviving baby, with a birth weight of merely 8.6 ounces—barely over half a pound! Born in Chicago at Loyola University Medical Center on September 19, 2004, Rumaisa was only twenty-five weeks, six days old at the time of birth. Her fraternal twin sister, Hiba, was 1 pound 4 ounces at birth.

Courtney and Chloe Smith made history by having the lightest combined birth weight of twins when they were born on March 1, 2000, in Louisiana. At birth, their combined weight was only 1 pound 8.5 ounces. Courtney weighed a mere 12 ounces and Chloe weighed 12.5 ounces.

statistics are facts, but it's important to remember that medical statistics on death and disease often represent a broad range of circumstances and do not necessarily apply to your specific situation.

Pregnancy with twins does carry a greater risk of complications. Yet staying positive has both emotional and physical benefits. Psychological stress and anxiety can cause the release of stress-related hormones, which can stimulate uterine contractions and place mothers at risk for preterm labor. An optimistic, positive perspective results in happier mothers and healthier babies.

Modern medicine has not only produced more twins but also resulted in more favorable outcomes for twins. The next time an unnerving twin story has you shuddering, here are some inspiring facts to focus on instead:

- There are more twins born now than ever before. This means that health providers have more experience in caring for twins than at any other time in history.
- Over 95 percent of twins with birth weights 1,500 grams (about 3 pounds 5 ounces) or more will survive.
- Over 95 percent of twins born twenty-eight weeks or more will survive.
- Over 80 percent of twins born after twenty-eight weeks will have no major newborn complications.
- The vast majority of twins born over 1,500 grams (3 pounds 5 ounces) will suffer no major disabilities.
- The youngest baby ever to survive was only twenty-one weeks, six days at birth.
- The smallest baby to ever survive was only 8.6 ounces at birth.

#4: Find Out If Your Twins Are Identical or Fraternal

In a 1998 reported medical case, a pair of twin brothers were diagnosed by physical characteristics as fraternal. When the one twin subsequently needed a kidney transplant, his brother happily donated a kidney. Because their DNA was thought to be different, the recipient twin took immunosuppressive medications to prevent his body from rejecting his brother's kidney.

Imagine their surprise when DNA testing fifteen years later proved the twins were identical. After years of taking powerful, immunosuppressive drugs with the assumption that their genetic composition was different, the recipient twin was able to stop all medications.

This story illustrates the importance of knowing whether twins are identical or fraternal early in life, if not prenatally. Because identical twins have similar genetic material, they are the ideal donors for each other in medical circumstances requiring blood transfusions or organ transplants. Similarly, genetic diseases that might manifest in one identical twin require consideration for testing in the other.

Most parents want to find out if their twins are identical or fraternal. Doctors, however, have traditionally been hesitant to distinguish identical from fraternal twins because of the potential for inaccurate diagnosis before and even after birth.

Dramatic improvements in ultrasound resolution and technique now allow increasing reliability in the prenatal classification of twins. Several features that can show up on ultrasound can be used to predict if twins are identical or fraternal:

TWIN FACTS *Differences Between Identical and Fraternal Twins*

Identical Twins

+ Also called monozygotic twins
+ Form when one egg and one sperm join and then split into two
+ Have matching DNA (the same genetic fingerprints)
+ Typically look similar, but not always
+ Always share the same gender
+ Occur in 1 in 250 births and comprise 30 percent of all twin pregnancies

Fraternal Twins

+ Also called dizygotic twins
+ Come from two different eggs fertilized by two different sperm
+ May theoretically be conceived at different times (and even from different fathers!)
+ Do not have identical DNA
+ May or may not look alike
+ May be different genders
+ Occur in about 1 in 30 births and comprise 70 percent of twin pregnancies

Rarer kinds of twinning can occur. Mutations in a baby's DNA after fertilization and other rare events may lead to more unusual variations in twinning. However, the vast majority of twins are either identical or fraternal as described in this book. In triplets and other high-order multiples, a combination of identical and fraternal twinning may occur.

- *A shared placenta.* Twins who functionally share a placenta are almost always identical. Features of the dividing membrane (membrane separating the babies) and evidence of connecting blood flow between the babies help determine if there is a shared a placenta. In the first trimester, doctors can tell with close to 100 percent certainty whether twins share a placenta by examining the dividing membrane. This accuracy decreases as the pregnancy progresses, however.
- *A shared fluid sac.* If twins share a common fluid sac (amnion), they are identical twins. After eight weeks of gestation, it is possible to determine if there is a separating membrane between the two babies or if they share a fluid sac.
- *The sex of the babies.* If twins are of the opposite sex, they are invariably fraternal twins.

After birth, examination of the placenta can help distinguish between identical and fraternal twins by confirming whether there was a shared placenta or fluid sac.

Even with prenatal ultrasound and laboratory examination of the placenta, roughly 25 percent of identical twins will still be missed because they have separate placentas like those found in all fraternal twins. Physical features may help distinguish identical from fraternal twins, but are known to be unreliable because identical twins may actually appear different and same-sex fraternal twins may look very much alike.

The most definitive way to determine if twins are identical or fraternal is to perform DNA testing, often referred to as *twin zygosity testing.* Identical twins have similar DNA and fraternal twins have different DNA. DNA testing compares two babies' DNA to determine if they match.

TWIN FACTS *Looks Can Be Deceiving*

Most people assume that the world's most famous twins, Mary-Kate and Ashley Olsen, are identical twins because they look so much alike. They are actually fraternal twins.

Although DNA testing can be performed on babies prior to birth, the risks associated with prenatal testing preclude this test from being done unless the babies' cells are collected for other reasons. Prenatal testing is also not as accurate as testing after birth because of the potential for sampling errors.

After birth, DNA testing is quite easy. The babies' cheek cells are collected for testing by rubbing a brush or swab inside their mouths. This is a painless procedure, but it can be fairly expensive (currently around $150 or more). Experts agree that

TWIN FACTS *Twins from Different Birth Mothers*

We typically think of twins sharing the same womb. But that is no longer always the case! I know of at least two sets of twins who were born by different mothers. How can that be? The embryos of a single couple were implanted at the same time into their biological mother and a surrogate mother. To the parents' delight, both babies survived, resulting in twins in different wombs. Technology continues to adjust our definition of "twins."

testing cheek cells is superior to testing blood cells because blood from twins can have mixtures of their DNA. The accuracy of DNA testing has been reported to approach 100 percent.

T I P #5: Take Steps Early to Know If Your Twins Share a Placenta

Twins who functionally share a placenta are called *monochorionic twins*. The most important reason to know if your babies share a placenta is that these twins require special medical attention. Yet a shocking survey of practicing obstetricians showed that many lacked adequate knowledge about the risks and management of these twins. Because of this knowledge gap, some physicians treat all twins in the same way. This is an inadvertent but dangerous practice that parents must watch out for in order to secure the best medical care possible for their twins.

Ask your doctor right away if your twins functionally share a placenta. The sooner your doctor looks for this on ultrasound, the more accurate the answer will be. If your twins share a placenta, this tip was written just for you.

The Special Risks of a Shared Placenta

One of the most important reasons you and your doctor should find out if your twins functionally share a placenta is the risk of *twin-to-twin transfusion syndrome (TTTS)*.

Twins who share a placenta commonly have blood vessel connections between them, and these connections typically retain a reasonable balance of blood flow to and from each twin. However, in TTTS, the blood flow between the twins becomes imbalanced. The placenta sends too much blood to one baby and too little to the other. One twin can become overloaded with blood while the other becomes anemic. TTTS is a dangerous situation that requires close monitoring and treatment.

Babies who share a placenta have a 15 percent risk of TTTS. Left undetected and untreated, the risk of death for one or both twins can be as high as 100 percent.

Reducing Your Babies' Risk of Twin-to-Twin Transfusion Syndrome Complications

The good news is that the majority of babies will never have TTTS. Even better news is that with close monitoring and modern treatments, babies with this condition have a better chance of survival than ever before.

To reduce your risk, many obstetricians recommend the following for all twins who share a placenta:

+ Involvement of a maternal-fetal specialist
+ Ultrasound in the first trimester
+ Ultrasounds every one to three weeks beginning in the second trimester (the TTTS Foundation recommends weekly ultrasounds from 16 weeks of gestation onward)
+ More frequent ultrasounds if there are abnormalities suggestive of TTTS
+ Maternal self-monitoring for signs of TTTS

If your babies are diagnosed with TTTS, contact the TTTS Foundation right away (www.tttsfoundation.org). The foundation not only dispenses valuable information to families but also provides financial assistance to those in need. Many healthy babies have resulted from the support of the TTTS Foundation.

Other Risks of a Shared Placenta

The placenta can be likened to the refrigerator in a home: it supplies all the food that a baby needs for growth and survival. A shared food supply means an increased risk for various complications, such as:

- *Intrauterine growth retardation (IUGR).* This term denotes poor growth in unborn babies. When two babies share a "refrigerator" with a limited food supply, they are at risk of not growing as well as babies with their own exclusive food supply.
- *Discordant growth.* When twins share a placenta, their umbilical cords can connect to the placenta unequally. This can result in one baby having more access to the shared "refrigerator" and growing bigger than the other. When the weight difference between the babies reaches 20 to 25 percent, they are considered to have significant discordant growth. These twins need close monitoring to ensure the smaller baby does not fail to grow due to insufficient access to nutrients.
- *Preterm birth.* Twins with a shared placenta are more likely to be born prematurely than twins with their own placentas. TTTS and poor growth are two factors that contribute to the increased risk of preterm delivery in twins who share a placenta.

+ *Monoamniotic twinning.* Some babies who share a placenta are also enclosed in the same fluid sac (monoamniotic). These babies share not only the same "refrigerator" but also the same living space. Because there is no membrane to separate them, their umbilical cords can become tightly entangled, cutting off blood flow to one or both babies. These babies require strict medical surveillance and often early delivery to prevent complications.

If your twins share a placenta, you and your doctor will need to closely monitor for the presence or development of any of these potential problems. Prompt diagnosis and intervention have been shown to have a positive effect on the health of babies affected by these complications.

The Power of Knowledge

The information in this tip can seem scary at first; but rather than let it worry you, use it to empower you. Remember, the majority of babies who share a placenta never experience any major problems. Nevertheless, understanding the potential risks of a shared placenta permits parents to assist in the early detection and treatment of any complications that may arise. By reading this tip, you have already given your twins the significant health advantage of an informed parent.

TWIN FACTS *Signs of Twin-to-Twin Transfusion Syndrome*

Every parent with twins who share a placenta should know the ultrasound features that screen for TTTS. You should ask your doctor about the presence or absence of these features at every ultrasound visit:

+ *Deepest pocket of amniotic fluid around each baby.* The normal amount is 3 to 8 centimeters. If the pocket of fluid is more or less than this range, it may be a sign of TTTS.
+ *Weights of the babies.* If babies have more than a 20 to 25 percent weight difference, they require close monitoring.
+ *Bladder size.* Marked differences in bladder size or the inability to see one twin's bladder may be a sign of TTTS.
+ *Signs of body swelling or heart thickening.* These may be signs that one twin is getting too much blood flow.

Between ultrasounds, look vigilantly for signs of TTTS. Call your doctor immediately if you experience any of the following possible symptoms of TTTS:

+ There is a sudden increase in weight gain.
+ Your abdomen feels suddenly tight and uncomfortably stretched.
+ The movement of one or both babies seems less than normal.
+ Your hands or feet swell early in pregnancy.
+ You feel contractions before your due date.

T I P #6: Get the Results of Every Test You Undergo

Physicians consider pregnancy with multiples a high-risk pregnancy. To prevent complications from going unchecked, mothers of multiples typically undergo many more appointments and tests than mothers pregnant with singletons.

Unfortunately, many pregnant women have no idea what tests are performed on them, much less the results. Physicians do not always tell mothers about test results unless something appears abnormal.

In a twin pregnancy, some tests routinely performed on single babies have little proven interpretative value in twin pregnancies. Also, there are tests that should commonly be carried out in a twin pregnancy that are not necessary in a normal singleton pregnancy.

It's important to ask your doctor about your test results for the following reasons:

- *Knowing the results of your tests makes you a better patient.*
  You will be able to tell physicians, especially in an emergency (before the medical records arrive), if you had any abnormal test results during your pregnancy.
- *Knowing the results of your tests can give you reassurance.*
  Some test results that could be interpreted as abnormal in singletons can be completely normal in twins.

- *Knowing the results of your tests makes you an active participant in your twins' care.* If you know what tests have and should be performed, you can ensure that such tests are completed during your pregnancy.

The next time your blood is drawn, your cervix is swabbed, or your abdomen is covered with blue ultrasound gel, remember to ask your doctors what they are looking for and be sure to write down every result.

Twin Story
Abnormal Second-Trimester Screen

With Faith and Hope, I was shocked when my second trimester screen for Down syndrome came back abnormal. However, knowing that routine screening blood tests for Down syndrome can have unreliable results in twins helped me decide against further, more invasive testing with amniocentesis. The thought of a needle being inserted into their fluid sacs and the increased risk for miscarriage associated with the procedure just didn't sit well with me. Faith and Hope do not have Down syndrome, and I'm glad that I did not expose them to any added risk.

TWIN FACTS *The Twin Factor in Prenatal Tests*
for Chromosomal Abnormalities

Routine tests for chromosomal abnormalities such as
Down syndrome do not always have the same predictive
value in twins, and sometimes they carry more risks.

Test	What Is It?	Trimester Tested	The Twin Difference
Nuchal trans-lucency	Ultrasound measurement of fluid behind the neck of the fetus. Increased fluid may be a sign of Down syndrome or other chromosomal abnormalities. Best noninvasive screen for chromosomal abnormalities in twins.	First trimester: between 11 and 14 weeks.	In twins who share a placenta, an abnormal test may be due to early TTTS rather than chromosomal abnormalities. Either way, close monitoring is needed.
First-trimester biochemical markers screen	Test that measures specific pregnancy-related substances in the blood. Abnormal levels can be seen in babies with chromosomal abnormalities.	First	Mostly used in twins in combination with the nuchal translucency test. Not as reliable when used alone.

Test	What Is It?	Trimester Tested	The Twin Difference
Chorionic villous sampling	Testing of a piece of the placenta to directly look at a baby's chromosomes.	First	Risk of cross-contamination (other twin's cells contaminate the specimen) or duplication (same twin tested twice).
Quad test	Blood test to screen for spinal defects, abdominal wall defects, and chromosomal abnormalities.	Second	Difficult to interpret in twins. Some medical centers no longer perform this test in twins.
Amniocentesis	Testing of amniotic fluid (fluid around the babies) to look directly at a baby's chromosomes.	Second	Each twin's fluid sac needs to be tested. Greater risk for contamination, duplicate sampling, and miscarriage than with singletons.
Second-trimester ultrasound	Screens for major birth defects. Certain findings, such as a heart defect, increase the likelihood that a baby has a chromosomal abnormality such as Down syndrome	Second	Can sometimes be technically more difficult with two babies.

TWIN FACTS	*Routine Tests Performed During Most Pregnancies*	
Test	**What Is It?**	**Trimester Performed**
Blood type and antibody screen	Blood test to determine your blood type and screen for your body's potential to inadvertently attack your baby's blood cells.	First
Hemoglobin	Blood test for anemia.	First; may be tested more often with twins due to a higher risk of anemia.
Hepatitis B surface antigen	Blood test for infection with hepatitis B virus.	First
Rapid plasma reagin (RPR)	Blood test for infection with syphilis.	First
Rubella antibody	Blood test to see if you are immune to German measles.	First
HIV antibody	Blood test to see if you are infected with human immunodeficiency virus.	First

Test	What Is It?	Trimester Performed
Urinalysis	Urine test to screen for a variety of conditions, including diabetes, infection, and preeclampsia (a serious condition characterized by high blood pressure and protein in the urine).	Typically done at every office visit.
Pap smear	Swab of the cervix to check for cervical cancer.	First
Chlamydia and gonorrhea testing	Swab of the cervix to test for infection with chlamydia and gonorrhea (sexually transmitted diseases).	First; this test is routine in many but not all centers.
Quad test	Blood test to screen for spinal defects, abdominal wall defects, and chromosomal abnormalities.	Second
Urine culture	Urine test to screen for infection.	Second
Ultrasound	Ultrasound examination to look for major birth defects.	
Glucose tolerance test	Blood test to check for gestational diabetes (pregnancy-associated high blood sugar).	Third
GBS screen	Vaginal sample to screen for infection with Group B streptococcus.	Third

TWIN FACTS *Nonroutine Tests That May Be*
Performed with Twins

Twin pregnancies require careful monitoring and often require special tests that are not routine in singleton pregnancies.

Test	What Is It?	Trimester Performed	Results
Frequent prenatal ultrasounds	An imaging test that uses sound waves to look inside the womb. Normal, singleton pregnancies typically only have one ultrasound. Twins need ultrasounds more frequently.	One in the first trimester. Then every three to four weeks for twins with separate placentas and every one to three weeks in twins who share a placenta. May occur even more frequently if abnormal findings are found or if the fluid sac is shared.	First-trimester ultrasound mainly done to determine if twins share a placenta or fluid sac. Genetic screening also offered. Second-trimester ultrasounds look for major birth defects and monitor for growth. For twins who share a placenta, doctors will look for signs of TTTS.
Doppler of umbilical blood vessels	Looks at blood flow patterns through the umbilical blood vessels for signs of abnormal flow.	Second trimester onward. Typically used if there are signs of poor growth or concerns for TTTS.	Babies with abnormal blood flow patterns require close monitoring.

Test	What Is It?	Trimester Performed	Results
Cervical length	Ultrasound measurement of the length of the cervix. Typically performed by placing an ultrasound probe into the vagina. A shortened cervix may indicate an increased risk for preterm delivery.	Second trimester. Performed every ultrasound from the second trimester onward.	A cervix that is rapidly shortening or 25 to 30 millimeters or less requires close monitoring and possibly medical intervention.
Fetal fibronectin	Tests for risk of preterm delivery. A swab for cervical secretions sent to look for this protein, which is seen up to a couple of weeks before delivery.	Third trimester	Normally absent (negative). A negative result is reassuring that delivery will most likely not occur within two weeks.
Nonstress test (NST)	Monitors placed on the mother's abdomen record contractions and a baby's heart rate patterns.	Third; frequency depends on risk factors such as signs of poor growth or the presence of a shared placenta or fluid sac.	Abnormal heart rate patterns may indicate fetal distress (a sick baby or a baby at risk for becoming sick). Frequent contractions may signal preterm labor.

(continues on next page)

| | | Trimester | |
Test	What Is It?	Performed	Results
Biophysical profile (BPP)	An ultrasound test combined with a nonstress test. Looks at a baby's heart rate, breathing, movement, tone, and surrounding fluid. Each normal factor gets 2 points for a total of 10 points.	Third; frequency depends on risk factors such as signs of poor growth or presence of a shared placenta or fluid sac.	As long as the fluid volume is normal, a score of 8 to 10 is considered normal.

TWIN FACTS *Nonroutine Tests That May Be Performed with Twins*, continued

#7: Tell Your Doctor What You Fear the Most

Don't be embarrassed to express your concerns to your doctor.

Parents want to protect their children from harm. After a child's birth, most parents usually do not have a problem with expressing their concerns regarding their child. However, prior to birth, many mothers feel embarrassed telling their doctors their fears and worries. This hesitation stems from the fact that many well-meaning mothers do not want to appear overly anxious or to inconvenience their doctors.

I advise every mother to view any worries in their pregnancy as concerns regarding their babies and not just themselves. Taking this perspective will allow you to freely express your concerns for the sake of your babies, even when you might not have wanted to ask for yourself.

Use these recommendations to keep the lines of communication open between you and your doctor:

- Before every office visit, write down a list of any questions or concerns you may have. Ask these questions during your visit, and write down the answer so you can refer to it later if necessary.
- If your doctor uses any medical terms that you do not understand, ask for an explanation of their meanings.
- When you read medical articles or online resources, feel free to discuss them with your doctor.
- If your doctor is short on time or cannot answer all your questions during your visit, ask if you can e-mail your questions and have him or her call you back with answers.
- Obtain your physician's contact number and use it liberally, even after office hours. Many offices have nurses who answer the initial calls, respond to common questions, and relay urgent matters to the doctor on call.
- Ask if your doctor has an e-mail system for asking and answering questions. This works well for nonurgent questions like, "Can I drink caffeinated products during pregnancy?" E-mail should not be used for communicating urgent matters. You need a direct conversation with a health provider if you have immediate medical concerns.

+ If you cannot reach your doctor and you have an urgent concern about the health of your babies, go to the nearest emergency room, where you can have an examination and live conversation with a physician.

T I P #8: Build an Experienced Medical Team

As the last few tips have shown, twins require specialized care. You need the right people to provide that care. One of the biggest mistakes parents can make is choosing an inexperienced medical team to care for their twins.

Virtually every medical insurance plan considers twin pregnancies "high risk." If insurance companies, which have every incentive not to pay for a higher level of care, consider your pregnancy worthy of close medical attention, you should take their word for it. Take advantage of whatever benefits increase as a result, and choose a medical team that will provide you with the best care for your babies.

Pregnancy Providers

A variety of health providers, including general obstetricians, family practitioners, and midwives, can provide excellent care to pregnant women. However, every twin pregnancy requires the involvement of a maternal-fetal specialist (also known as a *perinatologist*). Maternal-fetal specialists have specialized training in caring for pregnancies with the greatest risk for complications, including twin pregnancies. All perinatologists have four years of specialized training in women's health and pregnancy care after medical school. In addition, they have three extra years of focused training in the care of high-risk pregnancies.

It makes sense that if your twin pregnancy is considered high risk, you should have the involvement of a physician with expertise in managing high-risk pregnancies.

Newborn Providers

A high-risk pregnancy also warrants the involvement of a pediatrician who is trained to care for high-risk newborns—a neonatologist. Advances in the medical care of sick and premature babies have had a substantial impact on the overall survival of twins.

When choosing a birthing location, don't make the mistake of choosing a place simply because it has nice delivery rooms or luxurious amenities. The ideal hospital also has the facilities to care for your newborns should you deliver early or should medical complications arise.

If you have a choice, select a hospital with a Level 3 or higher neonatal intensive care unit (NICU). These units provide high-level care to premature babies and newborns with serious medical diseases. University medical centers and children's hospitals typically have Level 3 NICUs. Research has shown that extremely sick or premature babies have the highest chance of survival when born in hospitals with Level 3 or higher NICUs.

If no nearby hospitals have a Level 3 NICU, discuss with your obstetrician ahead of time how your babies can be quickly transferred to a Level 3 NICU if the need arises. It's important to have a plan set far in advance. Your babies may never need the care of an NICU, but it's better to be prepared for the possibility just in case.

The Team Approach

You do not have to change your current health care provider the instant you read this tip. Rather, I recommend adding more providers to your care if needed. For example, your doctor can work together with a perinatologist to provide optimal care for your unborn babies.

As a physician, I know the benefits of working on a team. When I see patients in the hospital, I lead a team of doctors and medical students. I may ask nurse specialists, nutritionists, child life advisers, social workers, therapists, and other physicians to consult in the care of my patients. Each health care specialist brings a unique perspective and set of skills that benefit the patient. Knowing the advantages of multiple providers, I chose a team approach for my own pregnancy.

The Most Important Team Member

You are the most important member of any team. Whatever combination of health providers you choose, your active participation is vital to the health of your babies. You should feel free to openly express your concerns and opinions regarding the care of your babies.

You will know you have chosen the right medical team when you find specialists who support your involvement and view your pregnancy as high risk enough to provide the close attention and specialized health care you deserve.

Twin Story
The Team Approach in Action

With Faith and Hope, I faced a number of pregnancy complications, including bleeding, cervical shortening, poor fetal growth, gestational diabetes, abnormal blood tests, and preterm labor. Believe it or not, there were even more complications not listed here!

Throughout my pregnancy, I had the choice of staying with my obstetrician or transferring completely to the care of a perinatologist. Each time, I decided that the best medical care for my children would be to see both.

I saw my obstetrician for my scheduled checkups. Every two to three weeks, I saw the perinatologists at my regular ultrasound appointments. Prior to my delivery, I was hospitalized for cervical shortening and preterm labor. My obstetrician and the perinatal team participated in planning my hospital care. When I delivered, my obstetrician happened to be out of town, and the perinatology team stepped in to deliver my babies.

The team approach continued after the birth of Faith and Hope. The obstetricians had done a great job of caring for Faith and Hope before birth, but now it was time for the pediatricians to play their role on the team. Fortunately, I had prepared myself for the possibility that Faith and Hope would need specialized newborn care by choosing an experienced pediatric team.

(continues on next page)

Faith and Hope came early, at thirty-three weeks. Faith showed serious signs of prematurity, including troubled breathing, which prompted ventilator support. Both babies had difficulty nippling and initially required feeding through a tube. Watching the respirator machine breathe for Faith, I was very happy I chose to deliver at a center that had not only a strong obstetrics team but also an exceptional team of pediatricians who specialized in the care of premature babies.

TWIN HINTS
When to Proceed with Caution

Beware of any doctor who says, "Relax, they're just twins." With triplets and quadruplets on the rise, some doctors have become overly complacent when it comes to twins. They may view a twin pregnancy as completely routine. Twins, however, especially ones who share a placenta, can have even more complications than some triplets.

Chances are that this doctor will be right and your twins will fare just fine. However, being a pediatrician who teaches others how to care for very ill children, I can tell you that what sets the best doctors apart from mediocre ones is the ability to see potential danger in even the most innocuous-appearing situations. Your doctor must view your pregnancy as high risk enough to look carefully for signs of complications. Although you don't want a high-strung doctor who will alarm you at every visit, you also don't want one who doesn't take your pregnancy seriously.

T I P #9: Lie Down on Your Side as Much as Possible

Obstetricians typically support continuing regular exercise for most pregnant women. However, this recommendation does not extend to mothers of multiples. In fact, many obstetricians recommend reduced activity for women pregnant with twins.

Don't be confused by resources that say bed rest should not be routinely prescribed in twin pregnancies. Although there is plenty of research on bed rest in singleton pregnancies, there are very few solid studies on this issue in twins. The boldest statements against bed rest refer to routine hospital bed rest—automatically being admitted to the hospital to reduce your risk of preterm delivery. Despite the controversy among doctors about bed rest, common sense combined with medical research supports at least some level of reduced activity for many pregnant mothers of multiples:

- *Reduced activity increases the availability of nutrients to your babies.* Twins need all the calories they can get in order to grow. It makes sense that if you are burning fewer calories, there are more calories available for your twins. Research shows that reduced activity does result in bigger babies at birth.
- *Lying on your side (especially with your left side down) increases blood flow to your babies.* When a pregnant woman stands or lies on her back, her enlarged, pregnant uterus can compress important blood vessels, resulting in decreased blood circulation to her unborn babies. Lying down on

your side increases blood flow (and subsequent nutrient flow) to your babies.

- *Reduced activity can reduce contractions.* Physical exertion and prolonged standing may increase contractions and a woman's risk for preterm labor. Women who are pregnant with twins should not engage in any aerobic exercise.

- *A reclined position relieves pressure from the cervix.* The cervix is the narrow passage at the lower end of the uterus through which a baby exits at birth. It typically stays long and closed to keep babies inside the uterus until the pregnancy has reached full term. In a twin pregnancy, the weight of two babies means a greater load on a woman's cervix. Lying down reduces the effects of gravity, relieving pressure on the cervix.

The more risk factors associated with your pregnancy, the more likely your doctor will prescribe some form of reduced activity. Pregnancies complicated by preterm labor, pregnancy-associated high blood pressure, a weakened cervix, poor growth, or TTTS often will result in stricter forms of bed rest.

Even if your doctor does not formally prescribe bed rest, I still encourage every mother of multiples to implement a self-imposed regimen to increase rest in her daily routine. Although there are certainly temporary inconveniences in decreasing your level of activity, the benefits to your babies may last a lifetime. Here are some easy ways to introduce more rest into your day:

- If you don't have to stand, don't. Sit down or lie down as much as possible.

- If you work, ask to have a reduction in job duties that require standing or walking in exchange for tasks that you can do while sitting (or even lying down).
- If you work night shifts, ask for temporary day shifts. Women who work day shifts typically get better sleep. Research suggests that women who work night shifts have a higher risk of preterm labor.
- If possible, eat while you work. Then use breaks and lunch time to lie down and even nap if you can.
- Whether at work or at home, schedule rest periods into your day—blocks of time specifically for you to lie down on your side and relax.
- Listen to your body. Your body is speaking for your babies. If you feel tired, stop what you are doing and sit or lie down.

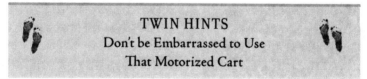

TWIN HINTS
Don't be Embarrassed to Use That Motorized Cart

Bed rest does not have to mean banishment from the outside world. Some doctors place mothers of multiples on modified bed rest, which often means you can get around on a wheelchair or a motorized cart. Many stores now have motorized shopping carts for use by their customers. At first, I was embarrassed to use the cart, but then I learned to enjoy the time it gave me outside the home. It also allowed me to purchase important items for my babies, helping me to feel productive and satisfying my nesting instinct.

TWIN HINTS
Ten Tips for Surviving Bed Rest

1. Gather a group of rotating visitors to assist you and keep you company.
2. Join online communities with mothers on bed rest. Sidelines at www.sidelines.org can match you up with a volunteer who can support you throughout your pregnancy by calling or e-mailing you.
3. Use this time to read. Read all the books you have been putting off. Read parenting books and magazines now, since you will have less time to read after the birth of your babies.
4. Borrow or buy a laptop computer. You can use a laptop to surf the Internet, keep a journal about your pregnancy experiences, or watch movies without having to get up from bed.
5. Get a bedside refrigerator or cooler. Your family can stock it with food and drinks so you don't have to go far when you are hungry or thirsty.
6. Use a number of pillows or a body pillow. Remember that you need to lie down on your side, not your back. Pillows propped in front of and behind you make staying on your side easier.
7. Ask your doctor about some light, nonaerobic stretches you can do in bed to keep your circulation flowing and your body from becoming achy and stiff. Poor circulation from inactivity can lead to the formation of dangerous blood clots. So it's very important to ask your doctor for ways to prevent this complication while on bed rest. If your doctor doesn't have suggestions, ask if you can consult a physical therapist for ideas.

8. Try a new hobby. You can learn to knit and make a blanket for your twins. You can read some books on digital photography and prepare yourself for all the great picture opportunities you will have with twins. You can watch videos on sketching and draw along. Any hobby you can do in bed will keep your mind active and make the time pass more quickly.

9. Create a schedule for yourself with goals for the day, just like you would before you started bed rest. That way, you can focus on your daily goals and feel productive during this time. Examples of goals include writing in your journal each day, finishing the quilt you started, or reading another chapter in your favorite book.

10. Remember that every day of bed rest means another day for your babies to grow inside you. Each day has a tremendous impact on their long-term health.

T I P #10: Negotiate a Long Maternity Leave

In the previous tip, I discussed ways for increasing rest in your work day. When your work environment simply cannot accommodate enough rest for your specific pregnancy needs, you may have to ask for a leave of absence.

At twenty-eight weeks, Faith and Hope were not growing normally, and my cervix had suddenly shortened substantially. When my doctor told me that I would have to go on strict bed rest, I was floored.

Like many other working mothers, I took pride in my job and my career achievements. Leaving my work responsibilities to another person did not come easily. However, when I looked at what would grant me the most long-term happiness—work success or ensuring the birth of healthy babies—the choice became simple.

Even if your doctor allows you to work, I recommend that all women who are pregnant with twins strongly consider negotiating time off from thirty-two weeks onward. Twins, on average, deliver at about thirty-six weeks. During the last weeks of your pregnancy, your body will appreciate the rest, and you will appreciate the time to prepare yourself for your twins' homecoming.

Here are some keys to maintaining a healthy pregnancy and a healthy relationship with your employer:

- *Honesty is the best policy.* Let your employer know that you are pregnant with twins. Those you work with will be much more sympathetic to your situation if they know they are helping you protect the health of your two babies.
- *The early bird gets the worm (or at least an appreciative boss).* Tell your boss that you are pregnant with twins and that sometimes that means an early or prolonged maternity leave. This will give your employer time to prepare for your absence. You can enthusiastically offer to use the time you have left to help train someone for your job duties.
- *Keep your doors open.* Let your supervisor know that you are willing to be available by telephone or e-mail to answer questions from those who are temporarily covering your duties. If your company doesn't think you are going to completely abandon your job, your boss will find it easier to

TWIN HINTS
Disability Insurance

If you are undergoing in vitro fertilization and are not yet pregnant, sign up for disability insurance the next time your company offers it.

Disability insurance covers a portion or even all of your salary while you are on bed rest. After the birth of your twins, you will continue to receive payments for several weeks while you recuperate from the delivery.

Many women who are pregnant with twins are prescribed some form of bed rest. If you consider that you may be out of work for up to several months prior to the birth of your babies, the salary support that comes from disability insurance will likely far outweigh the amount of money you paid into the plan.

Most insurance companies will not cover women who are already pregnant when they sign up for disability insurance. So if you are pregnant, be sure to find out if the insurance company excludes pregnant women prior to signing up.

happily support you while you are gone—even if your leave stretches out longer than you had expected.

- *More is better than less.* Even if you don't think you will need so much time off, it doesn't hurt to negotiate a longer leave now. It is always easier for your boss to give you more work than less. If you prepare your supervisor for the time off, you can decide to work or not when the time comes.

- *Seize the moment.* Consider taking the longest maternity leave protected under the law and that you can financially afford. After the birth of your twins, you and your body will appreciate the time to recuperate and adjust to caring for twins. Your twins will appreciate the bonding time they have with you during these precious early weeks of their development.

T I P #11: Let Your Own Home Get Messy, But Keep Your Baby's Home Sparkling Clean

If your doctor has you on bed rest, I know from experience that enforced relaxation can make you feel helpless and nonproductive. Here you are, not only stuck at home but also stuck in bed!

The natural reaction is to create work for yourself by attending to house duties when you should be attending to bed rest. This is not the time to have a spotless home. Rather, see your body as your babies' home. Let your house get messy, and focus instead on keeping your babies' home safe and clean.

For some women, the recommendations in this tip will come very easily. For others, it will present a major lifestyle change.

Know that your effort means a great deal to your babies. Giving your babies a happy, healthy home in the womb will benefit them more than anything else you do during this time.

Here are some important ways to keep your babies' home safe and clean:

+ *Eat nutritiously.* What you eat determines what your babies eat. Read Tip 12 for how to maintain a healthy diet.
+ *Avoid smoke exposure.* Smoking or inhaling second-hand smoke prevents babies from getting the food and oxygen they need to grow normally. The result is a greater risk of miscarriage and poor fetal growth. Twins already have a greater risk for poor growth due to competition for space and nutrients. Smoke exposure compounds such stress.
+ *Avoid toxic substances.* Alcohol and recreational drugs are toxic to babies. Avoid them completely. Check with your doctor before using any kind of medication, including over-the-counter medications. Even herbal medicines can have potent chemicals that can lead to birth defects and miscarriage.
+ *Stick to your prescribed bed rest.* Bed rest does not mean staying home and doing chores. It does not mean running a home office. It means a reduction in physical and mental stress for you and your babies.
+ *Consider going green.* I recommend that every mother read Dr. Alan Greene's book, *Raising Baby Green* (2007), for ideas on how to give your babies a clean, organic, environmentally-friendly start to their lives.

T I P #12: Don't Go on a Diet

The current trend in obstetrics is to minimize pregnancy weight gain. However, this does not apply to twins. In twin pregnancies, a mother's weight gain plays a crucial role in the health of her twins. Inadequate weight gain in a twin pregnancy increases the babies' risk of poor growth and premature birth. When it comes to twins, the bigger, the better.

How Much Do I Have to Gain?

You should gain at least thirty-five to forty-five pounds during your pregnancy. For an average-sized woman, the recommended starting point is about 2,700 calories a day.

You need to eat enough to gain roughly four to six pounds during the first trimester and one and a half pounds every week during the second and third trimesters.

If you are underweight or not gaining adequate weight, or your babies show signs of poor growth, your caloric goal may be even higher. If eating more does not result in adequate weight gain for you and your babies, your doctor may prescribe bed rest. By decreasing your energy expenditure, the balance of calories remaining for your babies' growth increases.

What Should I Eat?

You should aim to eat the following every day:

+ Three or more servings of dairy such as milk, yogurt, or cheese
+ Three or more servings of fish, meat, poultry, nuts, beans, or eggs

Twin Story
Eating for Three

During my pregnancy, Faith and Hope grew well until around twenty-six weeks, when Hope's growth dropped off. I was put on bed rest and told to consume more calories.

Around the same time, I was also diagnosed with gestational diabetes (pregnancy-associated high blood sugar). This meant that I could no longer eat a lot of carbohydrates like bread or pasta to increase my calories.

Initially I had a hard time figuring out what I could eat without causing my blood sugar to skyrocket. Fortunately, my obstetrics group had a nutritionist and physician assistant who specialized in dietary counseling for pregnant mothers.

Eating became my job. I was told to stop working, go on bed rest, and eat, eat, eat! And that is what I did! I made it my full-time job to grow my babies. I planned nutritious meals, checked my blood sugar as directed, and ate as much as I could.

With bed rest and proper nutrition, Hope's growth improved. By the time she was born, she surprised everyone by being bigger than anticipated. As a pediatrician, I was thrilled to know she was over 1,500 grams (3 pounds 5 ounces)—a benchmark weight above which the risk of long-term complications drops dramatically.

I know from experience that bed rest and meal planning can become a chore. But the benefits for your babies are worth it. See a nutritionist, plan your meals, and eat, eat, eat!

+ Four or more servings of vegetables
+ Three or more servings of fruit
+ Nine or more servings of bread, cereal, and pasta

Depending on your specific situation, you may be required to eat more or less from each food group. I recommend keeping a record of what you eat and reviewing the food diary with your doctor or a nutritionist. Continue logging your food intake until you have a solid idea of what you need to eat to meet your dietary requirements.

In addition to eating a variety of foods, be sure to drink at least eight to ten cups of fluids a day. When cooking with oil, select oils that are high in essential fatty acids such as sunflower, canola, and soybean oils.

How Often Should I Eat?

I recommend breaking up your caloric intake into three meals and three snacks. That way, your blood sugar remains stable throughout the day, resulting in a steady flow of nutrients to your babies.

As your pregnancy progresses, your enlarging uterus can press on your stomach, making you feel full sooner and increasing your risk of heartburn with large meals. Eating several small meals and snacks prevents you from having to consume huge amounts of food at a time.

Vitamin Supplements

Discuss any vitamin supplements you plan to take with your doctor or a nutritionist. It's important that you receive the right amount of vitamins without overdosing yourself. Eating a healthy diet will provide the majority of your daily vitamin requirements.

In addition to a well-balanced diet, the Institute of Medicine recommends the following supplements starting after twelve weeks of pregnancy:

- Iron: 30 mg
- Zinc: 15 mg
- Copper: 2 mg
- Calcium: 250 mg
- Vitamin B6: 2 mg
- Folate: 300 mcg
- Vitamin C: 50 mg
- Vitamin D: 5 mcg or 200 IU

Seeing a Nutritionist

Because twins carry a high risk of low birth weight, most insurance companies cover at least a one-time consultation with a nutritionist for women who are pregnant with twins. Research shows that women who received counseling from a nutritionist during their pregnancy had bigger, healthier babies. I recommend that every woman take advantage of a nutritionist consult if one is available.

TWIN FACTS *Foods to Avoid*

Certain foods that may be innocuous to most people
can be dangerous for pregnant women and their
unborn babies. Avoid these foods during pregnancy:

+ *Raw or undercooked meats, eggs, poultry, and fish.* When raw,
  these items can lead to infections with bacteria and parasites.

+ *Unpasteurized soft cheeses, homemade cheeses, and any
  unpasteurized milk products.* These may contain a dangerous
  bacteria called Listeria.

+ *Unheated deli meats, hot dogs, and leftovers.* Thoroughly heat
  these food items to avoid infection with bacteria.

+ *Large fish such as tilefish, shark, king mackerel, and swordfish.*
  These contain high levels of mercury, which can cause damage
  to an unborn baby's nervous system. The Food and Drug
  Administration (FDA) recommends eating up to twelve
  ounces a week of seafood lower in mercury, such as shrimp,
  canned light tuna, salmon, pollock, and catfish. See the FDA's
  Web site for more information on safe seafood consumption:
  www.epa.gov/waterscience/fishadvice/advice.html.

+ *Large amounts of caffeine.* Keep your intake to less than
  150 mg per day. Larger amounts have been linked to higher
  rates of miscarriage and low birth weight. Caffeine content
  can vary depending on how a beverage is made. Limiting
  yourself to one cup of coffee, tea or caffeinated soda a day
  will help keep you below this limit.

^TI^P #13: Bond with Your Unborn Babies

I fell in love with Faith and Hope from the moment I saw their beating hearts on ultrasound at seven weeks of gestation. Emotionally bonding with them before birth prepared me for the physical endurance that was required to take care of them after birth.

It's never too early or too late to form healthy attachments with your babies. At every stage of your pregnancy, there are ways you can strengthen your mother-twin bonding:

- *Name your twins.* As soon as you find out you are pregnant with twins, name them. Naming takes them from the unfamiliar realm of "embryo," "fetus," or "twins A and B" and places them immediately in your heart as your children.
- *Look at them.* At every ultrasound, ask for a picture of your babies. Looking at these images will remind you just how real they truly are. Line the images up and see how much they develop over the course of your pregnancy. These are your babies growing before your eyes!
- *Read, talk, and sing to them.* Research shows that newborn babies recognize their mother's voice from birth as a result of hearing it while they were in the womb. Verbally communicating with your unborn babies bonds you to them. Hearing your voice bonds them to you.
- *Touch them.* Place your hands on your belly and feel their kicks. Lightly press on your belly, and you may feel a kick in response.
- *Keep a pregnancy journal.* See Tip 14 for what to write in it.

T I P #14: Keep a Pregnancy Journal

Even if you don't consider yourself a writer, I encourage every mother to keep a pregnancy journal. You can use a bound notebook, a three-ring binder with blank sheets inside, or a commercially prepared journal with fill-in-the-blank questions.

A pregnancy journal will benefit you and your babies during your pregnancy. Use a journal to:

- Write your loving thoughts about your babies.
- Record inspiring quotes, words, and stories.
- List great tips you want to remember from books you have read and from other twin mothers.
- Track milestones in your pregnancy. Record events you would want to remember, such as when you found out you were pregnant with twins and when you first felt your babies kick.
- Express your fears and concerns. Putting your thoughts on paper relieves anxiety, thereby reducing stress hormones that can trigger preterm labor. Psychologists routinely recommend journals as a strategy to reduce stress in their patients.
- Organize questions for your doctor. Bring your journal to your appointments.
- Record your ultrasound and lab results. I kept a record of Faith and Hope's ultrasound growth measurements. It inspired me to see them go from being just a few ounces to several pounds.

After the birth of your twins, this pregnancy journal will serve as a precious keepsake for you and your babies. Your writings will detail for your twins how much you loved them from the beginning, even before they were fully formed. It will remind you of the challenges you faced, how you endured, and how you achieved a miraculous accomplishment in giving birth to twins.

T I P #15: Remember That Humor Can Help Overcome All Obstacles

Good humor is the key to maintaining a positive view of a unique pregnancy experience. There are many benefits of a good laugh. Here are a few:

- Laughing relieves stress, reducing your risk of stress-related preterm labor.
- Laughing releases endorphins—natural, pain-relieving chemicals. It also distracts your mind away from pain. I found laughter to be an effective, risk-free way to alleviate the nausea I suffered during the first half of my pregnancy.
- If you are relaxed, your babies will be more relaxed. When a women is upset, her unborn baby's heart rate rises in response to her distress. Your happiness translates into a more relaxed environment for your babies.
- Happy mothers are better able to bond with their unborn babies, forming an important foundation for a healthy parent-child relationship.

CHAPTER 2

Delivery

#16: Ask About Delivery Options Early

The average twin pregnancy lasts 35.2 weeks, whereas the average singleton pregnancy lasts 38.7 weeks. Because of the typical shortened time frame of a twin pregnancy, I recommend talking with your physician about your delivery options as early as 20 weeks.

Little research exists on the best mode of delivery for twins. Even with healthy twin pregnancies, complex factors come into play. The positions of the babies, the size of the babies, and the experience of the obstetrician all contribute to the decision-making process. The safest mode of delivery for one set of twins may not apply to another set of twins.

If you have a complicated pregnancy or one that requires an emergency delivery, cesarean section may be the only feasible option. However, if you have a healthy, uncomplicated pregnancy, vaginal delivery may still be possible, provided a number of factors are met:

+ *Both twins have their heads turned down, pointing toward your pelvis.* Until more research becomes available, many doctors will still attempt vaginal delivery if both mother and twins are healthy and if both twins are head-down, a position known as *vertex-vertex.*

+ *Ultrasound monitoring is available during labor.* Ultrasound allows the doctor to see if the babies' positions change and to respond quickly to these changes. If a baby moves from being head-down (that is, becomes *nonvertex*), a doctor may need to reposition the baby, deliver the baby feet-first, or perform a cesarean section. Ultrasound also allows a doctor to look at a baby's heart if the external heart monitor loses connection due to a moving baby.

+ *There is setup for an emergency caesarean section.* Even if you deliver vaginally, you need to be in a hospital with the setup available for an emergency cesarean section in case complications arise.

Some doctors may offer vaginal delivery if the first baby is head-down and the second baby is not (a *vertex-nonvertex* position). The nonvertex twin may be *breech* (feet- or buttocks-down) or *transverse* (lying sideways). Babies who are breech or transverse have an increased risk of getting trapped in the birth canal or having their blood supply cut off by a compressed umbilical cord. These births require physician expertise in delivering nonvertex babies. Therefore, not all doctors offer vaginal delivery for vertex-nonvertex twins.

Most physicians advise against vaginal birth if the first twin is nonvertex or if the babies share a fluid sac. For these twins, the risk of entrapment or compromised blood flow in a vaginal delivery is too high compared to a cesarean section delivery. If your babies fall into this category, you will most likely give birth by cesarean section unless your doctor has compelling reasons to the contrary.

Because every pregnancy is different, only open dialogue between you and your doctor can determine the best mode of delivery for you and your babies. Your opinion plays an important role in the decision-making process. Some women prefer to give birth vaginally if they have the option. Others elect for a cesarean section. These decisions are difficult to make, and trying to contemplate them during labor is next to impossible. Early discussion of what you and your doctor would want to do in each scenario (vertex-vertex, vertex-nonvertex, and so forth) will prepare you and your doctor for unified action on your delivery day.

T I P #17: Be Alert for the Signs and Symptoms of Preterm Labor

Preterm labor is defined as uterine contractions before thirty-seven weeks that result in cervical changes or other signs of imminent delivery. The bad news is that twin pregnancies have a sixfold higher risk of preterm delivery. An estimated 40 to 50 percent of all preterm births are preceded by preterm labor. The good news is that with early recognition, preterm labor can be slowed or even arrested with medications called *tocolytics*.

Each day that preterm birth is postponed can have a tremendous impact on your babies' health. If you go into preterm labor between twenty-four and thirty-four weeks, your doctor will give you a tocolytic medication to try to stop your contractions unless you or your babies are sick enough to require immediate delivery. Your doctor will concurrently administer a medication called a *corticosteroid*. This medicine will flow to your babies and will work to hasten your twins' development. If delivery can be delayed for at least twenty-four hours after the administration of the corticosteroid, your babies' risk of breathing difficulties, brain bleeds, intestinal inflammation, and death can be substantially reduced. By recognizing the early signs of preterm labor, you play a vital role in maximizing the health of you and your babies.

As someone who has experienced normal labor with a singleton baby and preterm labor with twins, I can attest to the fact that preterm labor can be very subtle. Many mothers who have had preterm labor state that they did not even know they were in labor until they saw contractions on a uterine monitor. Nevertheless, with a keen awareness of changes in your body, you can pick up signs of preterm labor before it progresses. Here are some symptoms to watch for:

+ Frequent or regular tightening of your uterus. Ask your doctor how many contractions per hour they consider significant. My doctor was called if I had more than six per hour or more than four per hour for two hours.
+ Abdominal pain or cramping.
+ Lower abdominal or pelvic pressure.
+ A sense that your baby is pressing down or dropping down into your lower pelvis.
+ Dull back pain or pressure.
+ An increase or change in vaginal discharge, especially if you see blood, mucus, or a trickling of clear fluid.

If you experience any of these symptoms, call your doctor immediately. Your doctor can help you decide the next steps to take. Even if it turns out to be a false alarm, it's better to be safe than sorry.

Twin Story
A Mother's Intuition

Contact your doctor if you sense your babies are ready to come out. Many mothers have told me they had a weird feeling they were going to deliver shortly before they did. It's not very scientific, but pay attention to this feeling.

During the last part of my pregnancy, I sensed that Faith and Hope were very close to birth. I had written the following passage in my journal: "I've told the doctors that my uterus feels very full, distended, and sore and that I feel a lot of pelvic pressure now, especially with contractions and ambulation. The larger twin's head is quite low and I feel her in my lower pelvis. The perineal pressure is great when I have contractions and stand up. This is how I felt 1 to 2 weeks before giving birth to Hannah. . . . My feeling is that I will go into spontaneous labor in the next 1 to 2 weeks."

I was hospitalized a day later due to a worrisome heart rate pattern on Faith and Hope's nonstress test and went into full-blown preterm labor just five days after that. Faith and Hope were born at 33 weeks—just about a week after my journal entry.

If there is one thing I have learned well as a pediatrician, it is that mothers are not always right, but they certainly are correct most of the time! Trust yourself, and don't hesitate to call your doctor if you think your babies are coming. You may very well be right.

#18: Don't Worry About Having a Picture-Perfect Delivery

When I gave birth to my first daughter, Hannah, I labored in a fully furnished, nicely decorated room. The television was on, and I watched contestants eat cockroaches on *Fear Factor* just prior to delivery. I had my husband and a room full of family members cheering me on.

With Faith and Hope, I gave birth in a chilly, sterile operating room even though I delivered vaginally. Medical staff filled the room, and my husband was the only relative allowed inside.

The typical twin delivery is anything but typical when compared to singletons. Nevertheless, it can be equally pleasurable provided that you know ahead of time what to expect. The more prepared you are for the unique delivery experience, the more you will enjoy the birthing process.

Here are several key differences:

+ *You will deliver in an operating room.* All C-sections and the majority of vaginal twin births are done this way. For vaginal births of twins, many doctors choose the operating room so that a C-section can be performed without delay if needed.
+ *You may see surgical tools.* Even as a physician, I found the surgical tools a little daunting from the patient end of the table. At one point during Faith and Hope's delivery, Hope was showing signs of distress, and I heard someone yell, "Get the scalpel ready!" The doctors never needed it, but I know it can be scary to see surgical tools laid out if you

have not prepared yourself mentally for the possibility of a C-section. I tried to see these shiny instruments as insurance rather than as a liability.

♦ *You will be surrounded by masked people—lots of them!* With a singleton delivery, your friends and family may fill the labor room. With twins, you will have a room full of medical professionals. Attendants may include an anesthesiologist, obstetricians, pediatricians, nurse practitioners, nurses, and respiratory therapists. Each person plays a special role in the care of you and your babies.

♦ *Your babies may be whisked away right after birth.* It is not unusual for twin babies to be delivered, shown to you, and taken to the room next door to be examined by a pediatrician. Some operating rooms have a warmer for the babies set up inside the room, and others have it outside the room. If your babies are premature or show any signs of breathing problems, they may be taken directly to the neonatal intensive care unit for further medical care.

TWIN FACTS *Largest Twin Babies*

The heaviest combined birth weight of twins is an incredible 27 pounds 12 ounces! On February 20, 1924, Mary Ann Ward Haskin gave birth to Patricia Jane, who tipped the scales at 14 pounds, and her brother, John, who weighed a sizable 13 pounds 12 ounces.

Delivering Faith and Hope was nothing like my birth experience with Hannah, but it was exhilarating and special in its own right. I had watched them grow from two undefined masses to two fully formed babies. Seeing Faith's lovely face and then Hope's five minutes later made the entire pregnancy experience worth it. The sound of two crying babies was like music to my ears. I never wanted to hear crying in stereo more than I did that day.

T I P #19: Take Lots of Pictures

Every hospital has a different policy regarding the use of video cameras in the operating rooms, so check with your doctor before filming during the delivery.

Nevertheless, most hospitals encourage picture taking. Remember to bring your camera to the hospital, keep the batteries charged, and take lots of photos when the time comes. With the flurry of activity associated with a multiple birth, you will appreciate the photos to look back on.

I recommend digital photography or videotaping for the mother's sake. Mothers, especially those who deliver by cesarean section, can have a limited view and memory of the birth process. Digital photos allow mothers to see the birth immediately afterward.

Remember, too, that the operating room will be crowded with medical professionals, so most relatives will be left outside the room. Taking digital pictures will make those waiting relatives happy in knowing they will get to see the birth pictures soon after.

Finally, your babies will appreciate the photographs one day. When they have grown, they will look back on these photos and see just how far they have come. These photos will bring to life the day you brought them into this world. The images will serve as a lasting reminder of your generous gift to them—your irreplaceable role in giving birth to them.

TWIN HINTS
Photo-Taking Tip

Make sure to keep blood and private parts in mind when taping or photographing a birth. If you would rather not remember these things, avoid capturing them on film since it's easy to forget during the excitement of a birth. And remember to review and edit your tapes and photos before sharing with others. I still recall being mortified by a three-second glimpse of my pubic hair projected on the screen as we shared our supposedly censored birthing video to relatives. If you'd rather your Uncle Bob and other family members not see these things, don't forget to edit them out before any major viewing.

T I P #20: Ask for a Private Room

Trust me: you will really appreciate this tip after you give birth to your twins. As a new mother to twins, you need all the space, privacy, and help you can get.

There are plenty of reasons for having your own room with twins. Here are the top ones:

- *You need physical space.* If your babies do not have to go to the intensive care unit, you will likely have them sleep in your room with you. Making room for two babies in a shared room often does not work well. You need the space that a single room provides.
- *You need bonding time.* You have two babies with whom to quickly acquaint yourself before you head home. Having a private setting allows you and your babies to maximally focus on each other during this critical time of early bonding.
- *You need emotional space.* Having your own room allows you to express your feelings uninhibitedly. Faith and Hope's beautiful birth was followed by a roller coaster of emotions from elation about their survival to despair over their initial health struggles. I was extremely thankful for a private sanctuary to openly express my thoughts and feelings during that time.
- *You need space to heal.* Even if you have an uneventful twin vaginal delivery, your body will typically need more time to recuperate than with a singleton delivery. Having a peaceful, comfortable place to rest will help with the healing process.

+ *You need help.* Many hospitals do not ordinarily allow another adult to spend the night in a shared room. You will want all the help you can get. You may need assistance walking around or caring for your two new babies. You will want your partner there to keep you company and to assist you in any way possible.

Tour the birthing hospital during your second trimester, and ask about the hospital's policy for room assignments. Ask if they automatically assign single rooms to mothers who have delivered twins. If the hospital allows you to reserve a private room for a small fee, I encourage every family to consider this important expense provided it fits within their budget.

If your hospital does not take advance reservations or does not automatically grant single rooms for twin pregnancies, politely inquire about a single room when you go into labor. Don't be shy about asking. If the rooms are not fully occupied, many hospitals will try to accommodate your request knowing that you have twins on the way.

TWIN HINTS
Dealing with Low Vacancy

If only shared rooms exist at your birthing hospital, make the most of the space on hand by asking for the largest room possible. If you have a choice, ask for the bed farthest from the door; you will see less hospital traffic and have more privacy. If your partner cannot stay in a shared room, ask if the hospital has any boarding rooms so your partner can be close by.

Although having a single room is ideal, don't fret if you cannot get one. What matters most is that you are in the best medical location to care for you and your babies. In the end, choosing the right hospital has much longer-lasting effects than choosing the right hospital room.

CHAPTER 3

The Neonatal Intensive Care Unit

The neonatal intensive care unit (NICU) is a special hospital ward that provides medical care for premature babies and sick newborns. Not every twin needs to stay in the NICU after birth. However, for a subset of twins, the NICU provides a temporary abode for healing and growing prior to their homecoming.

Tips 21 and 22 introduce parents to the NICU and apply to all families expecting multiples. Tips 23 through 26 address parents with babies in the NICU. Many twins bypass the NICU and go straight home. If this applies to your twins, you can skip Tips 23 through 26 and proceed to Tip 27 in Chapter Four.

#21: Visit the NICU During Your Second Trimester

Every family of multiples should take a tour of the NICU toward the end of their second trimester. Babies born between twenty-four and thirty-four weeks may spend several weeks to months in the NICU. Becoming acquainted with the staff and culture in the NICU will prepare you for your babies' potential stay there.

The People
Many different people provide care to babies in the NICU. Knowing each person's role helps make the NICU less intimidating. A typical NICU may host the following medical staff:

+ *Neonatologists* are pediatricians with three years of specialized training in the care of premature and sick newborns. They oversee the medical care of all the NICU babies.
+ *Pediatric hospitalists* are pediatricians who specialize in the care of hospitalized children. The pediatric hospitalists often

work in collaboration with a neonatologist in the care of NICU babies.

+ *Fellows/residents* are physicians who work under the direction of a neonatologist. Fellows are neonatologists in training, and residents are pediatricians in training.

+ *Neonatal nurses* provide the majority of bedside care for your babies. They are trained to care for the needs of premature and ill newborns.

+ *Neonatal nurse practitioners* are nurses with additional training in the care of NICU babies. They typically work in collaboration with a neonatologist.

+ *Respiratory therapists* perform treatments related to the lungs. They set up and make changes on the respirators and administer aerosol lung medications.

+ *Occupational and physical therapists* work with babies on their feeding and physical development.

+ *Social workers* specialize in providing social and psychological support to families.

+ *Case managers* help you plan for your follow-up medical care and equipment needs at home.

The Culture

Every NICU has its own policies. Knowing the culture of the NICU at your hospital will make assimilating into the environment easier. Common unit practices include:

+ *Scrubbing.* Before you enter the unit, you will have to stop by a sink and thoroughly wash your hands. This is done to prevent the spread of disease to newborn babies.

+ *More washing.* You will be instructed to wash your hands with soap and water or with an antibacterial gel when moving from holding one baby to another. You will also be instructed to clean your hands each time you subsequently want to hold a baby after touching anything else since last cleaning your hands.

+ *Visiting hours.* You and your spouse can visit anytime except two to three specific times a day when one shift of nurses is leaving and another is arriving. Other visitors can come only during designated visiting hours and only if they are with a parent. No children are allowed except for siblings.

+ *Illness.* Sometimes benign illnesses in adults such as a cold or a cold sore can cause devastating disease in sick or premature babies. If you are ill, you will need to check in with the NICU prior to visiting.

+ *Privacy.* The unit typically houses multiple babies in a large, shared room. For privacy, you can ask for a portable partition or screen while you are visiting.

+ *No adult beds.* You will not be able to sleep in the unit. However, you can rest assured that your babies will be cared for very closely by highly trained nurses at all times.

+ *Noise.* Although there appears to be a lot of background equipment noise, you will be asked to keep your voice no louder than normal level. Babies in the unit need a calm environment to rest, heal, and grow.

+ *Working as a team.* When you come into the unit, you will check in with the nurse caring for your babies. The nurse will give you an update on your babies and will help you feed, hold, and care for them.

T I P #22: Learn Some NICU Lingo

In addition to its own culture, the NICU has its own medical language for common conditions treated in the NICU. Doctors especially like to use acronyms in the NICU. Knowing the common medical terms will prepare you to discuss them with your doctor or other medical providers if the need arises:

- *Preemie*—a baby born prematurely at less than 37 weeks of age. The average twin birth occurs at 35.2 weeks. This is the most common reason for twins to require NICU admission.

- *RDS*—respiratory distress syndrome, a lung problem typically seen in babies born less than 34 weeks of age. Premature babies frequently have underdeveloped lungs that do not produce enough *surfactant*, an important substance that helps the lungs function normally. Babies with RDS often require oxygen and mechanical ventilation. Fortunately, doctors can give surfactant to babies with RDS. The availability of surfactant has dramatically improved the survival and health of premature babies.

- *PDA*—patent ductus arteriosus. Babies in the womb have a conduit between two blood vessels that stem from the heart. Usually, this conduit closes shortly after birth. When the conduit fails to close, this condition is called a patent ductus arteriosus. A PDA typically causes no major problems. However, it can sometimes lead to heart failure and breathing difficulties, especially in premature babies. In these cases, doctors can use medications or surgery to close the PDA.

- *NEC*—necrotizing enterocolitis, a condition characterized by inflammation of the intestines. Premature babies have a greater risk of developing NEC. Sometimes the intestines may be sufficiently damaged so as to require surgical removal of the damaged area.
- *IVH*—intraventricular hemorrhage, a bleed from small blood vessels in the brain. Babies less than 1,500 grams (3 pounds 5 ounces) have the greatest risk of IVH. Severe IVH can lead to neurological damage, but minor bleeds typically pose no major long-term problems.
- *ROP*—retinopathy of prematurity, a condition where the eye does not develop normally in premature babies. Some babies require laser surgery to prevent vision loss.
- *Hyperbilirubinemia*—a high level of bilirubin in the blood. Prematurity is one of the most common risk factors for hyperbilirubinemia. Premature babies do not process a normal chemical in the blood called bilirubin as efficiently as full-term babies. This chemical increases and causes yellow skin (jaundice). If severe jaundice is left untreated, bilirubin can build up in the brain and cause injury. Most babies with jaundice are easily treated by being placed under special fluorescent lighting that helps the bilirubin level drop. In rare cases, blood transfusions may be needed.
- *Apnea of prematurity*—long pauses in breathing in premature babies. Typically the brain automatically directs the body to breathe. The immature brain of a premature baby, however, sometimes allows the baby to stop breathing for too long. Treatment includes the use of medications to stimulate breathing. Premature babies typically outgrow

this condition once they approach the age equivalent to the number of weeks by which they were premature.

I know that reading about these conditions may be scary. The good news is that many of you will never hear these medical terms again. For those who do, use this information to arm yourself with knowledge. With a basic understanding of these conditions, you will have a better starting point for a more detailed and meaningful discussion with your doctor.

T I P #23: Feel Free to Cry

This tip begins with the assumption that your twins are in the NICU.

As a mother of preemies, I know that the NICU can be an emotion-wrenching place. Before their birth, you envisioned healthy, happy little twins dressed in matching outfits. Seeing your children on ventilators, hooked up to monitors, and requiring all kinds of equipment to feed them, breathe for them, and keep them warm can shatter your dreams and break your heart.

Yet I also know from experience as a physician that the NICU is a place of miracles too. It is like no other medical unit I have ever encountered as a doctor. Here even babies who are less than a pound can survive and then thrive. Of all the patients I have ever cared for, I am convinced that neonates are the strongest patients in the hospital. They can endure infections, lung injuries, brain insults, and trauma that would otherwise kill an adult.

Each year the NICU at our hospital hosts a picnic for all their NICU "graduates." It is truly amazing to see babies who were once tiny, sick, and premature now living and thriving.

If your babies end up in the NICU, know that many other parents have been in the same heart-wrenching situation. We truly feel your pain. Cry as much as you need to. I cried oceans seeing my babies so sick and so small. My heart reaches out to those of you who will be where I once was: standing over a warmer watching my baby fight for her life.

There is hope. In the haze of heartache and fear, look at that warmer sheltering your baby and feel the echoes of history under those shining lights. Where your baby lies, many babies have struggled, grown, and survived. Close your eyes, imagine all the graduates at the NICU reunion picnic, and hold on to your hope.

T I P #24: Remember These Are Still *Your* Beautiful Babies

You cared for your twins from the moment of conception. You did everything you could to give them the best chance possible for survival. And you gave birth to these two beautiful souls. Then suddenly, after months of being their sole provider and lifeline, your babies are cared for by doctors, nurses, and other staff. Sometimes they are so sick you cannot even hold them. You don't know what your role is in this setting.

It's easy to feel powerless in the setting of an NICU. However, you do have the power to care for your babies in ways that no one else can. You, in fact, are the most important member of the team. Here are some ways to get yourself actively involved in your babies' care:

- *Visit them whenever you can.* Remember that your babies know your voice from the time they spent with you in the womb. Even if they are too sick to hold, you can gently hold their hand and softly speak to them. Let them know you are there and that you love them.
- *Make sure you rest.* When your babies are in the NICU, it's easy to want to spend your entire life in the hospital. Certainly spend time with your babies, but also make time to rest. Rest allows your postpartum body to heal, restores your emotional energy, and helps increase your breast milk supply. Your rest is good for you and your babies.
- *Pump breast milk.* Breast milk is the perfect food source for babies and should be used if at all possible. Especially in the first days after birth, breast milk is rich in antibodies—proteins that help babies ward off infection. These antibodies are not available in formula. To maximize your milk supply, ask for a consultation with a breast-feeding specialist.
- *Keep informed of your babies' care.* Ask your doctor or nurse to give you daily updates on your babies. You can call to speak to your nurse if you cannot be physically present with your babies. Ask for clarification if you do not understand something about your babies' condition or care.
- *Educate yourself.* Use this time to ask questions and to read up on caring for your babies at home.
- *Ask to help.* Ask your bedside nurse how you can help care for your babies. Your nurse will engage you in their care through activities such as feeding and changing them.

+ *Hold your babies.* Ask if your babies are ready to be held under your shirt and next to your bare chest, a bonding position used in "kangaroo mother care." See Tip 25 for more information.

+ *Make something.* If you crochet or knit, you can make your babies blankets, booties, or hats. You can write them a card expressing your love, create a photo collage of your family, or sew them a quilt to put over their incubator. Put your energies into making something for your babies. It will serve as a wonderful keepsake for them in the future—a reminder of your outpouring of love for them through a challenging time in their lives.

T I P #25: Cuddle Like a Kangaroo

Over thirty years ago, Dr. Edgar Rey Sanabria found himself disheartened by the rate of newborn infections, abandonment, and deaths in his Colombian hospital. The hospital's supply of incubators and medical providers could not keep up with the overwhelming demand for these resources. This ingenious physician envisioned the concept of mothers serving as live incubators and active caregivers for their babies.

Dr. Rey began strapping babies vertically on their mother's bare chest and under her clothes. Like baby kangaroos who find food, warmth, and a safe place to grow in their mother's pouch, Dr. Rey's patients matured and thrived in their mothers' "pouch." This revolutionary life-saving concept came to be known as *kangaroo mother care* (KMC).

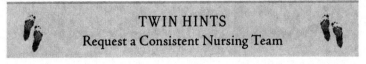

TWIN HINTS
Request a Consistent Nursing Team

Neonatal intensive care units provide care to babies twenty-four hours a day. Nurses work eight- to twelve-hour shifts. This means that in one day, your babies may be cared for by up to three different nurses. The total number of nurses caring for your babies may multiply tremendously if the same nurses are not assigned to your babies each day.

Request that the same set of nurses care for your babies every day if that is at all possible. The greater exposure a nurse has to your babies, the more knowledgeable she or he will be about your twins' specific needs and temperament. Nurse-infant bonding also increases with time and can have advantageous effects on your babies' overall care. Finally, it will be easier for you to get to know the nurses if they stay consistently the same. The more acquainted you become with the nurses, the more comfortable you will feel asking them questions, caring for your babies alongside them, and leaving your twins to their competent care when you go home each night.

Traditional KMC involved mother and baby remaining strapped to each other continuously. Mothers would carry their babies in a vertical position for twenty-four hours a day and would sleep in a semisitting position.

Today the plentiful availability of modern equipment in most countries has changed the practice of KMC in these settings from continuous to intermittent. In the United States, babies typically can start KMC once they are stable and off the ventilator.

Since Dr. Rey introduced KMC, researchers from around the world have investigated the effects of kangaroo care and have found these potential benefits to babies:

+ *Temperature control.* Your body provides a stable warming source for your babies. With KMC, babies remain warm without the need for any additional heating equipment. Some studies have also shown more stable heart rates and breathing patterns in babies receiving KMC.
+ *Improved breast feeding.* KMC increases production of breast milk while increasing the quality and duration of breast feeding.
+ *Noise reduction.* Your body and clothes shield your babies from outside noise. This reduces startling and promotes relaxation.
+ *Improved sleep.* You have a soothing effect on your babies. Babies are calmer and sleep better when kept in close physical contact with their parents.
+ *Bonding.* Holding your babies physically close to your heart has the powerful effect of bringing your hearts emotionally closer.

Of all the benefits of kangaroo care, one of the most important is the empowerment it gives to parents. When you hold your babies in the kangaroo care position, you truly feel empowered. You sense the comfort you are giving your babies. You feel their minds and bodies relax as you hold them. You feel your strength showering over your babies, giving them strength to grow. You intuitively know that this is something wonderful and beneficial for your babies. You are the most important person to your babies, even in the NICU. Kangaroo care helps you realize just how much.

TWIN HINTS
Rooming-In

A few days before your twins' expected discharge, ask your doctor about the option of rooming-in: boarding you and your babies together in a hospital room outside the NICU. During that time, you will live with your babies and provide full care for them while nurses are available to instruct and assist you. Not every family needs this transitional hospital care. But if you are new parents or if your babies have special needs, this is an option worth exploring.

#26: Find Out the Benchmarks for Going Home

Every child's situation is different, and parents should ask their medical team what criteria must be met before their babies can go home. Knowing the benchmarks for discharge will help you plan for your twins' special homecoming day.

In general, most NICU babies need to meet a number of goals prior to being discharged. These are the most common:

+ *Feeding.* With rare exception, babies must show that they can drink enough milk to grow without any problems with feeding.
+ *Weight gain.* Babies need to show a consistent weight gain of roughly 20 to 30 grams (about 1 ounce) a day. There is usually no specific final weight they must achieve prior to going home.
+ *Temperature control.* Your babies must maintain a steady body temperature without the help of an incubator. This typically means the ability to hold a temperature greater than 97.5 degrees Fahrenheit while lying clothed in an open crib.
+ *Normal breathing.* Most babies will not be discharged until they are off oxygen and breathing normally.
+ *Car seat capable.* Most NICUs perform a test to check your baby's breathing in a car seat. If your babies are too weak or small to safely tolerate the ride home, your doctors may advise more time in the NICU for them to grow.

+ *You feel ready.* We always make sure that parents feel prepared to care for their babies at home. Use your time in the NICU to learn all about your babies' care well in advance of their anticipated homecoming. That way, when your twins are ready to go home, you will be ready for them.

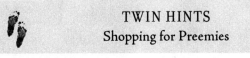

TWIN HINTS
Shopping for Preemies

Looking for preemie clothes but can't find any at conventional baby stores? Check out these great online stores:

+ The Preemie Store (www.preemiestore.com)
+ Nurture Place (www.nurtureplace.com)

Both sell a vast array of preemie attire, including NICU-friendly clothes that do not interfere with hospital monitors and equipment. I found Faith and Hope their "going home" and "welcome party" outfits at these sites.

CHAPTER 4

Sensible
Shopping

T I P #27: You Don't Have to Buy Two of Everything

Having two babies does not mean having to spend twice the amount of money. Twins can share many items, especially when they are infants. Before you buy or register for two of everything, take note of this list of items that your babies can share:

+ *Swings.* Most infants love being in a baby swing, but they also get bored in them after awhile. I recommend purchasing a variety of items to entertain them when you are unable to hold them. Instead of buying two swings, invest in a swing, a bouncy chair, and a play gym. That way, you can switch these items when a twin gets bored of one or the other.

+ *Baby carriers.* If you are alone with your babies for much of the time, you will not use two baby carriers often enough to make buying two of them worthwhile. Most baby carriers do not allow you to strap both carriers onto your body at one time. The ones that do are typically not comfortable for either you or your babies. I found that even with my husband around, we rarely used both carriers at once since we also had a stroller with us on most outings.

+ *Changing tables.* Never mind having two side-by-side changing tables. Even if you have another adult with you at all times, it won't hurt a baby to wait the few minutes it takes for you to change his or her sibling.

+ *Baby bathtubs.* You really only need one. When your babies are small, it's easier (and safer) to bathe one baby at a time, especially when you don't have another adult to help you during bath time.
+ *Toys.* Buy several different toys rather than two of everything. Your babies will like the variety, and having one of each toy will encourage sharing.

TWIN HINTS
The Twin Bassinet

Not buying two of everything will free up money to buy items that you really need. With the money you save, consider splurging on a twin bassinet.

This uniquely designed bassinet has two side-by-side sleeping compartments separated by a mesh partition. This allows your babies to sleep close to each other without clobbering or rolling over each other.

When your twins get fussy, you can put both in the bassinet and gently rock them to sleep at the same time. This trick worked like magic with Faith and Hope.

Although the twin bassinet costs more than a single bassinet, it typically costs less than buying two individual bassinets. When your babies outgrow the bassinet, it converts into a large playpen that accommodates two babies better than standard-sized playpens do. To date, Graco makes the only twin bassinet on the market. You can order one online through Babies "R" Us, Target, or Graco.

TIP #28: Pace, Not Waste

Huge mistake: loading up all at once on every baby item you think you will need.

As a mother of twins, I felt the need to stockpile baby supplies, not knowing when I would ever have another opportunity to shop. The problem with this shopping strategy became obvious later, when I came across things that had expired or that the babies outgrew before I could use them.

With the busyness of caring for twins, it's difficult to keep an accurate inventory of what you have. Buying in stages will help you keep organized, prevent clutter, and help prevent waste.

Key items to buy in stages include the following:

+ *Diapers.* Babies outgrow diaper sizes rather quickly, especially the preemie and newborn sizes. Newborns grow roughly 1 ounce a day—which means they gain about 1 pound every two weeks! I recommend buying diapers in one-month increments.

+ *Clothes.* It's easy to want to buy a lot of cute clothes for your twins, but it's better to buy them in stages so they don't outgrow them before they have a chance to wear them a reasonable number of times. Forget hoarding clothes for them that are months ahead in size. It's too easy to forget you have them.

+ *Food items.* When it comes to formula and baby food, buy enough for just a couple of weeks at a time—just like you do for your own meal planning. This prevents having to discard these items if your baby's taste or dietary needs change. Food items also expire, so buying food in stages will ensure the items you have bought don't spoil before you have a chance to use them.

+ *Toys.* Buy toys that are developmentally appropriate for your twins' current age. Don't load up on toys designed for older children since these toys may have features that are dangerous for younger babies. Locking these toys up in a safe place predisposes you to the risk of forgetting about them.

T I P #29: Look for Bargains

Raising twins can quickly add up financially if you spend frivolously, so mothers of multiples know how to bargain-hunt! Make it a habit to save when you can. Remember, you have eighteen years (or more) to shop for your twins!

These are some great money-saving shopping tips that I received from other mothers of twins:

+ Shop at your local mothers of multiples club's annual sale.
+ Consignment stores and thrift stores often sell clothes and furniture at low prices. Check them out. Just make sure items such as cribs are up to current federal safety standards.
+ Everything does not have to match. If you find an item for a good price, buy it even if they don't have two of the same item.
+ Shop at dollar stores and other discount stores.

- Buy frequently used items in bulk at warehouse stores such as Costco or Sam's Club. This is especially useful for nonsized items that your babies will not quickly outgrow, like wipes, baby shampoo, and lotion.
- Look for "buy one get one free" specials. These were designed just for twins!
- When others want to buy your twins something, ask for practical items such as diapers, wipes, and formula. Then you can save money to buy fun things for your twins, such as clothes and toys.

TWIN HINTS
One Item Not to Buy Used

One item I do not recommend buying used is a car seat. Car seats must meet current safety standards and not have a prior history of being in a car accident. It's a gamble with your children's safety to use anything other than a brand-new car seat.

If you decide to use a previously owned car seat, make sure you ask for and trust the history of the seat prior to accepting or purchasing it. Make sure the seat is in good condition. Remove the cover and ensure the foam and plastic are intact and not cracked. Straps should be clean and not frayed.

Register all car seats (even used ones) online with the manufacturer so you can receive notification of any updates or recalls specific to your car seat.

TWIN HINTS
Ask for a Twin Discount

Anh Tran, mother to twin boys, shares this hint: "Some baby stores may give you a discount if you buy two of the same things and you tell them you have twins. This usually applies only to big ticket items like car seats and strollers, but it never hurts to ask about other items too."

#30: Shop Online If You Can't Go Out

Prescribed bed rest or the busyness of caring for twins does not have to stop mothers from power shopping. The Internet provides a fantastic avenue for viewing and pricing merchandise.

Start with these tips for making your online shopping experience efficient and cost-effective:

+ *Create an online wish list.* You can create a wish list or baby registry at the store of your choice. A list lets you organize your shopping while allowing family and friends to know exactly what you still need for your babies.
+ *Batch your buying.* To avoid racking up multiple shipping fees from the same store, wait until you have several items you want from that store before placing an order.

- *Buy large items in the store.* Large items such as furniture can be very expensive to ship. For such large articles, consider making a list of items you found online and then asking a family member to shop for them at a local store.
- *Search for coupon codes.* Many online stores have promotional or coupon codes. Before purchasing an item, do a quick Google search with the store's name and the words "coupon code" and "promotional code." I have saved hundreds of dollars over the years by doing this five-minute search before every online purchase.
- *Become a registered member.* I do not recommend giving out your personal information or signing up for promotional e-mails from a lot of sites. However, if you often patronize a particular store, signing up for its e-mail promotions may save you money through deals such as a certain percentage off your purchase or free shipping.
- *Price search.* If you know what you want to buy, search for the best deal by visiting a price comparison Web site such as Buy.com. These sites provide not only the price of the item, but also the total cost with taxes and shipping included. You can also individually search your favorite stores for an item, but make sure to look at the total cost and not just the list price of the item.
- *Return policy.* Make sure a site has a good return policy before you make a purchase. I like sites that pay for return shipping or allow an item to be returned to a physical store.

TWIN HINTS
Internet-Based Stores for Mothers of Multiples

Currently, there are no popular chain stores that cater specifically to twins. However, several Internet-based stores sell items just for twins. My favorite online sites are listed below:

+ The Best Dressed Child (www.bestdressedchild.com). Fantastic place to buy matching boy-girl twin outfits.
+ Double Blessings (www.doubleblessings.com). Cards, keepsakes, and other items for twins and family members.
+ Double Up Books (www.doubleupbooks.com). Sells books on twins.
+ Ever So Tiny (www.eversotiny.ca). Manufacturers of preemie clothing and a nursing pillow designed especially for twins.
+ Just 4 Twins (www.just4twins.com). Adorable twin clothes and personalized items.
+ Just Multiples (www.justmultiples.com). Well-chosen, stylish items. I especially like the beautifully illustrated baby memory book, *Twice upon a Time: Twins Baby Memories* (2007).
+ Twinshoppe (www.twinshoppe.com). Sells a unique Two Peas in a Pod Diaper Cake: an array of diapers, baby necessities, and clothes batched creatively together to look like a cake.
+ Twinstuff Store (www.twinstuff.com/store/catalog). Sells a variety of twin items. I particularly recommend browsing the birth announcements and personalizable gifts section.
+ Twinz Gear (www.twinzgear.com). Great collection of items specifically for twins.

TIP #31: Put Safety First

When shopping for twins, don't forget to shop for childproofing supplies.

With multiple children in one home, it's easy to turn away from one child to attend to the other. Raising multiples makes a safe home environment all the more important.

As a pediatrician, I typically counsel my patients to child-proof their homes before their children become mobile—around nine months old. However, in the case of twins, I recommend getting the house safety-fitted as soon as possible. Once things get busy with caring for twins, the large task of childproofing a home can become quite difficult to tackle.

Making a home safe for twins can seem extremely daunting at first. Visit any child safety section in a baby store or on a Web site, and you can easily feel overwhelmed by all the products to prevent potential hazards in the home. Work one room at a time, and at a minimum, buy these important safety items:

- *Stair gates.* For multilevel homes, install gates at the top and bottom of the stairs. Use wall-mounted stair gates because pressure-mounted gates can buckle.
- *Safety netting or acrylic plastic sheets.* Buy mesh or acrylic plastic sheets to fill the open space between the railings of stairs and balconies.
- *Window guards and locks.* I recommend locks on all windows to prevent children from falling out of them. Consider window guards (also known as window gates) for all upstairs rooms and any other room where children may

go unattended for any period of time, such as their bedroom. Remember that window screens do not protect against falls.

+ *Childproof door knobs and locks.* Place on the door of any room you don't want your children to access. I recommend these on all bathroom doors and any doors that open to the outside of the house.
+ *Childproof gates.* Place in doorways and hallways to keep your twins away from unsafe areas in your home.
+ *Cabinet latches and locks.* Place all dangerous items in higher cabinets and shelves and then install cabinet latches and locks. Common hazardous items include medications, flammable items, cleaning agents, batteries, small items your babies can choke on, and sharp utensils.
+ *Stove knob covers and stove guards.* Install these to prevent burns and inadvertent carbon monoxide poisoning from a gas stove that is turned on but not lighted.
+ *Fire and carbon monoxide detectors.* Install at least one on every floor of the house, especially near bedrooms. Make a habit of checking the detectors at least once a month to ensure that they are functioning properly.
+ *Electrical outlet covers.* Cover all unused outlets to prevent electrocution. For used outlets, try to shield them with furniture. For plugged-in appliances, make sure the cords do not dangle in such a manner that a child can pull on them.
+ *Furniture anchors or straps.* Tall, heavy furniture should be secured to walls with anchors or furniture straps to prevent them from falling on top of children. Better yet, avoid tall furniture in children's rooms altogether.

- *Foam cushions.* Purchase self-adhesive cushions for sharp edges and corners on tables, desks, and fireplace hearths.
- *Door stoppers.* Replace door stoppers with rubber tips with one-piece plastic stoppers to prevent children from removing and choking on the rubber tips.
- *Hot water faucet covers and antiscald devices.* Install these to prevent water burns.
- *Toilet lid latches.* Install these to prevent children from falling head first into toilets and drowning.
- *Skidproof stickers or a tub mat.* Apply to the bottom of the bathtub to prevent falls.
- *Skidproof rug.* Place on uncarpeted bathroom floors to prevent slippage on wet floors.
- *Foam or inflatable bathtub faucet covers.* Use to prevent children from hitting their heads on the bathtub faucet.
- *Pool and spa hard covers, locks, and gates.* A fence should be installed around all bodies of water to prevent drowning. Fence gates should have self-closing hinge doors. In addition, I recommend self-closing hinges and an alarm for doors that lead to backyards with a pool or spa. Consider installing water disturbance alarms designed to detect water disturbance or displacement.

As you install these safety items, get down on your hands and knees to see things from the vantage point of your children. Watch your twins play in a particular room while keeping an eye out for potential hazards. By using these techniques, you will find childproofing needs specific to your twins and your particular home. Do this for every room before deeming that room childproof.

Although no child safety device can replace the need for continuous, close supervision by an adult, these items can add another barrier of protection against injury. Before you know it, you will see your twins outgrow these items. You will be thankful for the investment you made to get your babies safely to the point where they no longer need these protective measures.

TWIN HINTS
Create a Childproof Haven

With twins in the home, few families have the time to completely childproof a home all at once. To childproof your home in stages, I recommend focusing on one room at a time. You can restrict access to all unfinished rooms by placing childproof door knobs or gates to those unsafe quarters.

Start your childproofing project with the creation of one large, safe space for the babies to play. One practical mother of twins told me she gated off her entire living room. She removed all the furniture and made it into one big, childproof play area. If she needed to do something that required her to lose supervision of her twins for a brief period of time (for example, to use the bathroom or prepare meals), she could leave them in the playroom without much worry. If you have a large enough room, you can arrange a similar situation by purchasing an extra-wide or corral-type gate system to partition part of a room.

TWIN HINTS
Safe Practices

Here are some more tips for preventing accidental injuries in the home:

+ Avoid placing sofas or other furniture against windows to prevent children from climbing them and falling through the windows.
+ For lighting, consider ceiling or wall-mounted lighting. This prevents children from pulling a dangling cord and having a lamp fall on them.
+ Replace window treatments purchased before 2001 with newer, safer products. Older window treatments with cords pose a major threat of strangulation because they were manufactured before the institution of current cord safety standards. If replacement is not possible, visit the Window Covering Safety Council's Web site at www.windowcoverings.org/basiccordsafety.html for free retrofit kits to make older window coverings safer.
+ Keep household plants away from young children to prevent accidental ingestion. Even plants deemed "safe" can be poisonous in large amounts or cause injury if a child chokes on them.
+ Buy age-appropriate toys to avoid choking and other unintended injuries during play.
+ Reset your hot water heater thermostat to 120 degrees to prevent water burns.
+ Avoid bathing young twin babies together in a large tub while by yourself. Even when infants are able to sit, they can slip while sitting and fall with their faces below the water level. When you

have two babies falling underwater at the same time, it can set up a dangerous situation. If you must bathe them together, use a separate baby tub designed to safely support each baby rather than putting both in a large tub. One mother of twin toddlers recommended using two small laundry baskets.

+ Never leave young children unattended in a bathtub because they can drown in as little as two inches of water. If you decide to bathe your twins together, never leave one twin baby in the tub while you dry the other. Rather, take both babies out of the water, and then proceed to dry and dress them.

+ Lock up any weapons or firearms. Firearms should have a childproof gunlock or trigger lock. Store guns unloaded, and lock guns and bullets separately.

CHAPTER 5

Staying
Organized

#32: Be Sure You Can Tell Your Twins Apart

Tommy had a hole in his heart, and his identical twin brother, Timothy, had a normal heart. Before their discharge from the NICU, Tommy's doctor scheduled an appointment for him with a heart specialist to evaluate his need for heart surgery. At Tommy's follow-up appointment, an ultrasound showed that his heart had healed. Or had it? It turns out that Tommy and Timothy's parents had accidentally switched them. A quick ultrasound of "Timothy's" heart revealed a hole. "Timothy" became Tommy again, and he got the medical attention he needed.

As illustrated in this story, sometimes the misidentification of a twin can have serious consequences. In addition to the effects on their physical health, telling your twins apart can play an important role in their emotional development. Knowing one child from the other allows you to treat your children as unique beings. This, in turn, fosters their sense of individuality and self-worth.

Take steps to conclusively distinguish your twins from birth. I recommend fingerprinting all same-gender twins whether they are identical or fraternal. We typically think of identical twins as looking alike, but fraternal twins can look very similar too, especially as infants. By fingerprinting your twins right after birth, you can confidently refer to these fingerprints to identify them if any confusion later arises.

Fingerprints will help to accurately distinguish your children even if they are identical twins. Amazingly, although identical twins have similar genetic fingerprints (DNA), they have uniquely different physical fingerprints.

Many hospitals obtain hand and feet prints for security reasons. Ask about this option for your babies. If your hospital doesn't provide fingerprinting, you can buy a pad and fingerprint them yourself.

TWIN HINTS
The Beauty of Nail Polish

Use nail polish to help tell your twins apart. Assign a color to each baby, and paint their toenails their assigned color. So you don't forget who was assigned which color, label the polish bottles with their names.

I recommend painting toenails instead of fingernails since babies often like to suck their fingers. You can use this color-coding method on both boys and girls. If you don't want to paint all the toenails, painting just one will do just fine. Alternatively, you can paint just one twin's toenails and leave the other's unpainted. Use whatever discreet mark you think appropriate.

One great thing about nail polish is that it can last several weeks on babies without washing off. Plus, it comes in so many colors that you can have some fun with them. We have identical twins, and in the first weeks after their birth, nail polish helped set us straight on who was who many times!

The day you take your babies home, don't immediately remove their hospital bands. Keep the bands on until you feel you can easily tell your twins apart or have devised some other system of identification. These bands can last a couple of weeks at home. Remove them when you are ready, but before they fit too snugly.

While you acquaint yourself with the subtleties that distinguish your babies from one another, you can dress them in an assigned color. For us, Faith wore pink clothes, and Hope wore purple. A special knitted cap for each baby also helped us tell them apart quickly.

Consider keeping a notebook for each baby that lists his or her unique features. As your babies grow, continue to record any new distinguishing marks or traits. In our case, we noticed that Faith had a mole on her abdomen and Hope had one on her left foot. Our relatives quickly adopted this identification method and looked at their feet for the absence or presence of a mole.

Over time, most families do learn to detect subtle differences in their twins, even if they look very much alike. But I wouldn't count on that 100 percent of the time. I recently met a twin mother who introduced her children to me and then said to one of them, "You're Betty, right?" The two-year-old nodded. I don't blame this mother for having to double-check; her twins were extremely similar in appearance! But chances are that you will want a more foolproof system of identification. Start immediately at birth, and continue to document distinguishing features as your twins mature.

#33: Maintain a "Twin-Driven" Schedule

"Don't do things last minute. Plan ahead, and stay on a schedule," advises Anh Tran, the mother of twin boys. Heed these wise words!

A popular parenting technique today is the "baby-driven" schedule. Practitioners of this method feel that babies should never be put on a planned schedule. Although I support this mode of parenting for single babies, it often does not work well for twins—at least in early infancy. When you have two babies who feed every two hours and sleep only two hours at a time, the lack of a routine can make it very difficult for you to get any rest. As it is, families of multiples survive on very little sleep.

Compound lack of sleep with a chaotic schedule, and babies are bound to be double-fed or not fed at all, not changed or changed twice. When Faith and Hope were young infants, there were occasions when I lost track of time and had difficulty remembering when I last fed them. By maintaining a schedule, I could easily determine when their last feeding occurred and when

---

TWIN HINTS
Feeding Charts

For organizing meals, you may find a feeding chart useful. Create a chart for each twin and have dates and feeding times preprinted on the sheet. Then simply place a check next to each completed feed.

---

their next feeding was due since feeds occurred at the same time each day.

I recommend developing a "twin-driven" but nevertheless planned schedule. This means establishing a daily routine that works for you and your babies. You'll want to use your babies' cues to create a schedule that meets their particular needs. This is quite different from saying that every set of twins should be on the same, universal schedule. As your babies mature and their needs change, create a new routine to follow. Keeping a schedule requires discipline, but the effort benefits all parties in the long run.

 ## #34: Keep a Separate Journal for Each Baby

Most children one day ask about what they were like as babies. For twins, remembering each twin's milestones and unique moments helps them feel special and individually loved.

I recommend a blank baby journal or one with preprinted fill-in-the-blank questions and headlines. Buy one for each baby. You'll likely want to record precious memories such as:

- Their birthdays, birth weights, heights, and head circumferences
- Details of their birth: what you were thinking, how long you were in labor, your first thoughts when seeing them
- World events at the time of their birth
- Their homecoming story: when they came home, what they wore, who was home to greet them

- Their nursery: the design, the layout, if they slept together or in their own cribs
- Major developmental milestones: their first smile and laugh; when they rolled over, crawled, walked, and talked
- Details of their first taste of solids: what they ate, how it went, and their favorite foods
- Birthday party details
- Other key events, such as when they grew their first tooth, had their first haircut, and went on their first trip

CHAPTER 6

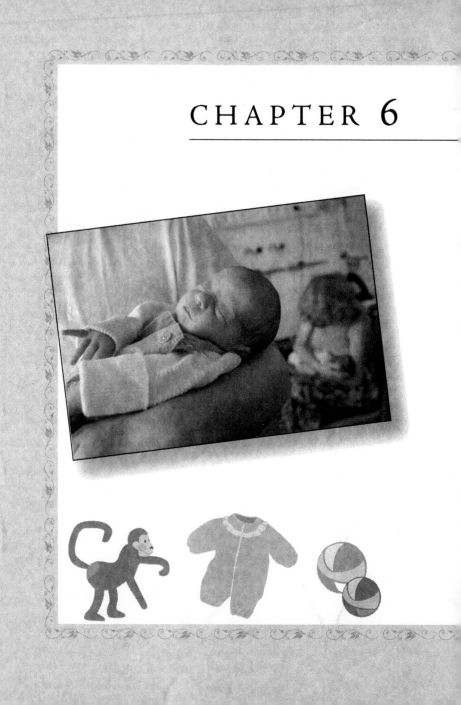

Feeding and Dressing Twins

T I P #35: Be Open to Different Nursing Techniques

Dr. Kimberly Douglas, a pediatrician and mother of twin girls, advises, "Be flexible in finding out what works for your family." Her advice sums up the point of this tip: the right way to nurse your babies depends on you and your babies' needs.

Many mothers of multiples choose to breast-feed. It may take some practice, but you can learn to breast-feed both twins at once. To make things easier, consider buying a nursing pillow made just for twins. This will help position your twins comfortably and keep you comfortable as well.

Some mothers prefer to breast-feed their babies one at a time. If you decide to do this, be sure to alternate babies between each breast so that one baby does not nurse from the same breast every time.

You can train most babies to feed one after the other by consistently feeding them thirty minutes apart. Scheduled, staggered feeding is a popular technique NICU nurses use when bottle-feeding babies.

Like breast-fed twins, bottle-fed babies can follow a staggered or simultaneous feeding schedule. Some mothers prefer to feed their babies one at a time so they can easily focus on each baby. Anh Tran, mother to twin boys, found that "feeding both at the same time was difficult. We actually staggered their feedings one after another. That may seem tedious, but that ensured that each child got individual attention and ate as well as he could."

While staggered schedules may work well for some families, some twins prefer simultaneous feedings. Faith and Hope came

TWIN HINTS
Bottle Feeding with Love

Breast feeding naturally creates an atmosphere for bonding. However, some babies cannot nurse on the breast for one reason or another. If your babies require bottle feeding, you can still create intimate moments of connection with your babies as they eat by using some of the following tips:

+ Feed your babies in a quiet place where there are no environmental distractions. That way, you can focus on each other.
+ Look lovingly at your twins.
+ Gently talk to them, and tell them that you love them.
+ You can softly sing to your babies while feeding them.
+ If feeding one at a time, hold your baby close, skin to skin, and gently stroke your baby's head or hand.
+ Don't feel bad if you wanted to breast-feed but were unable to. Remember that a mother's love for her babies is more important than any feeding technique. Your love will traverse any distance that a bottle may seem to create.

home on a staggered schedule, but it wasn't long before they made it clear that they wanted to eat together. Feeding presents a special opportunity to bond, and I found it impossible to bond with one baby while the other screamed throughout her sibling's entire feed. I learned rather quickly the art of bottle-feeding both babies at once.

You can easily bottle-feed your twins simultaneously by sitting each child in a car seat or bouncy chair. Make sure both babies are tilted upward at a thirty- to forty-five-degree angle and not lying flat. Face both seats toward you, offer a bottle to each baby, and . . . presto! Instant happy babies!

T I P #36: Feed Solids That Are Convenient and Developmentally Appropriate

Before you know it, your twins have reached four to six months of age and are ready for solids.

Starting foods is one of my favorite moments in parenting. A baby's transition from a purely milk-based diet to eating solid foods marks a key milestone in their lives. A baby's face covered up with food for the first time brings tears of joy to my maternal, sentimental soul. This momentous occasion reminds you that your twins are not tiny newborns anymore. They are growing up, and quickly! Eating opens up a whole new world of sensory exploration, social interaction, and motor development. These are precious times. Take lots of pictures!

When to Begin

You can start feeding your babies solids around four to six months of age. The American Academy of Pediatrics recommends waiting until at least four months of age to decrease the risk of developing food allergies. If allergies run in your family, your pediatrician may recommend waiting longer before starting solids.

Generally babies will tell you when they are ready for solid food through a number of physical and behavioral cues. Typically, it's best to wait until your twins have good head control and can sit easily with support in a high chair or on an adult's lap.

You will notice that your babies have started to show an interest in eating. They may stare at you while you eat. You may even see them smack their lips as they watch you eat. If you feel that they are watching your every bite, it may be time to get your children in on the fun! Just be sure they are physically and developmentally ready.

How to Begin

Many pediatricians recommend starting with rice cereal since it is generally well tolerated and one of the foods least likely to cause an allergic reaction. You can mix the rice cereal with breast milk or formula so the taste is familiar to your babies.

For your babies' first meal, you may want another adult to hold them (one at a time) in his or her lap while you feed. Alternatively, you can seat your babies in side-by-side high chairs and feed them both at once. Definitely have a bib on the babies. Things will get messy!

Using an infant spoon, offer a small amount of food at a time to your babies. It's completely normal and fine for your babies to push or spit out food at first. No worries. You can keep trying as long as your babies show interest and seem to be enjoying themselves. Signs that your babies are done with eating include turning away or shutting their mouths. End the meal at this point, and look forward to trying again the next day.

Once your babies eat rice cereal without difficulty for a couple of weeks, you can introduce baby-food vegetables. Offer one type of vegetable for a few days at a time so you can give each baby a chance to get used to the taste of a new food. This method also

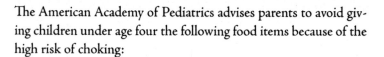

TWIN HINTS
Top Food Choking Hazards

The American Academy of Pediatrics advises parents to avoid giving children under age four the following food items because of the high risk of choking:

- Nuts and seeds
- Popcorn
- Whole grapes
- Hot dogs
- Raw vegetables or fruits that are not chopped completely
- Hard, gooey, or sticky candy
- Chunks of meat or cheese
- Chunks of peanut butter
- Any hard, rounded food item

allows you to detect the offending agent if one of them develops an intolerance or allergic reaction to a food item. Possible signs of food intolerance include vomiting, diarrhea, excessive irritability, or development of a rash.

Once your babies have tried a variety of vegetables, you can add fruits. Offer one new food item for a few days before adding another. You can also slowly increase solid-food feedings from one to three times a day over a period of several months.

When your babies can sit well alone and can pick up objects between their thumb and forefinger, you can introduce some finger foods. Babies typically reach this milestone anywhere between nine and ten months of age. Finger foods help strengthen your children's feeding abilities as well as their fine motor skills (finger dexterity and strength).

My favorite finger foods for babies this age include softly cooked, chopped-up vegetables such as carrots, pumpkin, and potatoes. Be sure to cook vegetables enough so that they easily mash with little pressure. Ripe, diced bananas are also popular at this age. Other favorites include well-cooked pasta pieces, baby cereal bars, and soft breads such as homemade cornbread, biscuits, or bran muffins. You can add foods such as soft tofu squares, grated mild cheese, and minced chicken for protein.

By around one year of age, many babies can obtain the majority of their nutrition through eating. You can offer chopped-up versions of your family meals at this age, provided that the food is soft or easily chewable. Formula-fed babies can start whole milk at one year as long as they are capably eating a variety of foods. You can also start moving away from bottles and make the transition to sippy cups at this age.

Take Your Time

As you feed your twins, remember that solid foods will not replace the important nutrition in breast milk and formula until they reach around twelve months. So don't feel rushed in advancing your babies on solids.

Continue to feed your babies breast milk or formula until they are at least one year old in order to ensure they are getting adequate nutrition while they learn to eat. Take your time introducing solids, and let your babies dictate their pace.

Take lots of pictures, and enjoy every moment!

TWIN HINTS
One Accessory You Can't Live Without

Shopping for your twins can be so much fun. But don't forget one vital item for yourself: a dark pair of sunglasses! I'm not kidding. While there are many times you will stroll leisurely and proudly around with your twins, occasionally you will want to breeze through a mall or grocery store without interruption. Don your glasses when you need to rush but don't want to brush aside well-meaning, curious gazers. Twins gather attention, and most of the time, you will love it. For the times when you need your privacy, you will be very happy I shared this tip with you!

T I P #37: Dress Them Alike If You Want To

Let's face it: people love seeing twins and love to see them dressed alike. And yet parents of twins often hear mixed messages about whether they should dress their twins in matching outfits. They think it's cute, but they have heard that they will harm their babies by stunting their individuality.

Let me take this moment to release you of all anxiety regarding this topic by telling you this: you will not scar your infant twins if you dress them alike. Indulge yourself in dressing your babies the same if you want to.

Once your twins approach two to three years of age, they will have a personal interest in their clothes and want to choose their own outfits. At that point, they should be allowed to choose if they want to dress alike or different. Before that age, feel free to dress your babies in whatever attire you think is best.

With Faith and Hope, we initially dressed them differently because we had a hard time telling them apart. However, once we could easily identify them by their physical features, we found dressing them alike had practical value (in addition to enhancing bragging rights). Clothing both twins the same simplified our dressing routine tremendously. For example, we didn't have to think twice (literally!) when choosing outfits or waste time deciding which garments would be put on which baby. We never had to consider whether one baby was dressed warmer than the other because their clothes were exactly the same. Finally, and maybe most important, having the same outfit helped us remember whose clothes had been changed and whose had not.

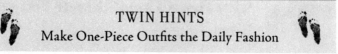

TWIN HINTS
Make One-Piece Outfits the Daily Fashion

As cute as twin babies look dressed from head to toe in coordinating outfits, most families find out quickly that putting together a four-piece outfit of shirt, pants, socks, and shoes every day becomes quite a task. Each item, especially shoes, adds an even greater level of complexity to the dressing routine.

Enter the one-piece outfit with sewn-in booties. Before your babies can walk, a one-piece outfit with booties provides a convenient, money-saving, and efficient mode of dress. A one-piece outfit in light cotton replaces shirt, pants, socks, and shoes. And a one-piece outfit in fleece replaces those four items *and* a sweater.

But wait, there's more! If you are concerned that your babies are cold at night, use a thick one-piece outfit instead of a blanket. The American Academy of Pediatrics recommends avoiding blankets in the bed to prevent sudden infant death syndrome (SIDS) in infants less than one year of age. One-piece pajamas provide not only a practical means of dress but a safe alternative to a blanket as well.

TIP #38: Consider Going Green

As a pediatrician, I have always been a proponent of organic foods and an earth-friendly way of living. The primary mission of a physician is to promote health and to prevent disease. What better way to do this than to feed our children chemical-free foods and give them a clean world to live in?

What wasn't so obvious for me as a mother of twins was how I was going to "go green" without going blue with exhaustion. How can a mother of twins grow an organic vegetable garden when she barely has enough energy to grow her own children?

As I read Dr. Alan Greene's *Raising Baby Green*, however, I realized that going green doesn't happen overnight. Going green is about taking one easy step at a time, and not about following a strict book of rigid behaviors to follow. It's about living a practical,

---

TWIN HINTS
Eating Green

According to Dr. Greene, here are some ways to jump-start a healthier diet for your twins while protecting the environment:

- Use organic formula and milk.
- Buy organic soy products.
- Use organic baby cereal.
- Buy or grow organic fruits and vegetables.
- Cook with organic meats.

healthier existence that is mindful of our impact on our health, our children's health, and the world we live in.

So am I growing an organic garden while chasing after twin toddlers? No, I'm not. Did I rip out all my flooring and replace it with organic bamboo? No, I didn't (not yet at least). One day, I do envision my children and me planting vegetables in my side yard. It'll be fun to do that and teach my children why. But until then, I'm going to make each day count by making one organic, environmentally friendly change at a time. I suppose you can say that I'm "growing greener" rather than "going green."

Living a greener existence makes sense. And it's possible with twins. Start your green journey by reading *Raising Baby Green*. As you read, focus on the simple steps that work for you and your family. Every change matters. Grow greener for you, your children, and our world.

TWIN HINTS
Dressing Green

Here are some earth-friendly ways to dress your twins:

+ Choose clothes made from organic fibers. Even large retailers like Target have organic clothing lines.
+ Avoid overbuying. You can prevent the waste of precious resources by reducing unnecessary redundancies in your twins' wardrobe.
+ Choose clothes that fit your babies but are slightly bigger at the start so they last longer.
+ Buy or accept offers of used clothing.
+ Recycle your twins' clothes by donating them to other mothers of twins or to charity.

CHAPTER 7

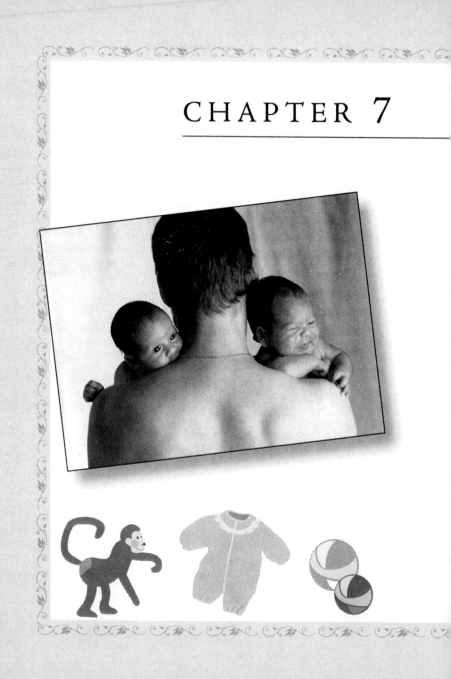

Sleep (or Lack Thereof)

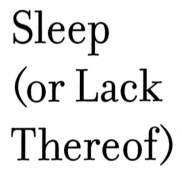

T I P #39: Divide and Conquer

Parents of multiples can consider a continuous eight hours of sleep a thing of the past—at least for the first four to six months after their twins' birth. That fact aside, you can maximize your hours of restful sleep by sharing nighttime duties with your partner.

Here are a few ways you can divvy up nighttime feedings:

+ *Split the night into shifts.* This allows each parent to sleep uninterrupted for a longer stretch of time. This method works well for twins who are on staggered feeding schedules.
+ *Assign one baby to each parent.* With Faith and Hope, my husband and I had to resort to this method because both babies would wake up simultaneously and cry. Even if the parent "off-duty" tried to rest, the hungry cries of the unfed baby made it impossible to sleep. By taking responsibility for one child each, we all ended up sleeping better.
+ *Ask for help.* Ask a relative, friend, or a hired nanny to take an overnight shift from time to time. Getting a full night's rest does wonders for renewing your energy.

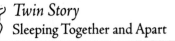

Twin Story
Sleeping Together and Apart

Here are two stories of how two mothers of twins handled their sleeping arrangements.

Anh Tran, mother to twin boys, said, "We kept the boys in the same bed until they were three months old. Then we separated them, but they were still in the same room. Even if one was a fussier sleeper than the other, keeping them in the same room trained them to sleep through each other's cries."

Kimberly Douglas, mother to twin girls, explained the solution she and her husband came up with: "We slept in separate rooms for sanity's sake until they were four months old. Steve would take the less cranky baby, and I would take the other one. After they were sleeping through the night, we were finally able to put them in their own room, and we were back in ours."

#40: Snuggle Them Close, But Snuggle Them Safely

Co-sleeping (or allowing your babies to sleep with you) has the potential benefit of increased bonding. It can also facilitate night-time feedings, especially if you are breast feeding or recovering from childbirth. Co-sleeping permits you to easily check on your babies or to comfort them when they cry at night.

Although co-sleeping has many advantages, bed sharing (sleeping with your babies on your bed) carries an increased risk of sudden infant death syndrome (SIDS). Rather than placing your babies directly in bed with you, I recommend using a separate but nearby infant bed.

You can reap the advantages of co-sleeping while minimizing the risk of SIDS through one of the following options:

+ *Snuggle Nest.* This unique baby bed was designed to be placed next to you on your bed. The Snuggle Nest keeps babies inside a padded, protective plastic frame. The bed cushion provides a comfortable but firm sleeping surface.
+ *Arm's Reach Co-Sleeper.* This bassinet attaches to your bed. The Original Co-Sleeper is big enough for a pair of twin babies. When your babies outgrow the bassinet, you can convert it into a playpen.
+ *Bedside bassinet or crib.* Simply pull a regular bassinet or crib up next to your bed for easy access.

Snuggle Nests, co-sleepers, and baby bassinets offer safe co-sleeping options until your babies are around three to four months old. At that age, they can roll over and risk falling out of

TWIN FACTS *SIDS Prevention Strategies*

Regardless of the infant bed you ultimately choose, safe sleeping means adhering to the American Academy of Pediatrics' guidelines for SIDS prevention:

- Place infants on their backs to sleep.
- Use a firm sleep surface such as a firm crib mattress.
- Avoid soft or loose objects in the bed, including blankets and pillows.
- Consider infant sleepers or sleep sacks as alternatives to blankets.
- Consider offering a pacifier to an infant who is ready to sleep.
- Do not smoke during pregnancy or around the babies after they are born.
- Provide a sleeping place for your babies that is near but separate from you.
- Avoid overheating.
- Allow your baby supervised "tummy time" while awake.
- Make sure all caregivers are educated on SIDS prevention.

these infant beds. I recommend moving twins to their own full-sized crib when they are around three months old—before they roll for the first time. The good news is that around this time, many babies require only one nighttime feeding, and some babies require none. You will find that the transition to cribs coincides well with your babies' changing needs.

T I P #41: Teach Healthy Sleep Habits

A cloud of persistent parental fatigue starts to lift the first time that twins sleep through the night. Parents of multiples uniformly cite this moment as a landmark event in parenting twins.

"Sleeping through the night" means a stretch of sleep of five hours or more. Many babies reach this milestone at four to six months of age, but variation exists among individual babies.

Every baby has an individual developmental time line, but you can prepare your twins to sleep through the night as soon as they are developmentally ready by teaching them healthy sleep habits in early infancy:

- *Keep daytime activities lively.* During the day, be active with your babies. Play with them, talk to them, sing to them, and give them plenty of eye-to-eye contact. This teaches them to be active during the day and not at night.
- *Avoid extended naptimes.* Newborns need naps, and it's vital to allow them to sleep during the day. As babies mature, they naturally nap less frequently. The important thing is not necessarily to limit naps but to avoid extended naps (those that last four or more hours). If your babies are

napping four or more hours at a time without waking up for a feed, you'll want to ease them into sleeping that long at night instead.

+ *Develop a bedtime routine.* Sticking to an evening routine helps signal to your babies that bedtime is approaching. Dim the lights, give them a bath, read them a book, sing their favorite lullaby, and institute any other bedtime tradition that you want to build into your nighttime routine. Whatever you do, make sure that it is easily replicated day after day.

+ *Let your babies fall asleep drowsy but awake.* When your babies seem drowsy but before they fall into a deep sleep, put them gently in their bed. If they wake up momentarily, you can pat them back to sleep. Try not to immediately pick up your babies if they cry when you put them into their bed. This teaches them to learn to fall asleep in their bed, not in your arms.

+ *Wait, then act.* Babies (and adults for that matter) naturally have periods of light sleep or brief awakenings during sleep. If you hear your babies fussing and it's not time for a feeding, wait a few minutes to see if they fall back asleep on their own. If the crying continues, then you'll want to check on them.

+ *Keep your actions minimal.* When you do go to your babies at night, make sure that your interactions are not overstimulating. Even if you need to feed or change them, keep the lighting dim, avoid eye contact, whisper or keep silent, and do not play with your babies during this time.

- *Know when all bets are off.* If your babies are sick, are in an unfamiliar setting, or you have any reason to suspect something is wrong, you should tend to them as you see fit. Sleep training should mainly focus on times when things are routine.
- *Avoid comparing yourself with your friends.* Remember that it's not bad parenting or your twins' fault if it takes longer than average for your babies to sleep through the night. With twins, prematurity and lower birth weight can delay their readiness for terminating nighttime feedings.

These tips are meant to encourage a pattern of healthy sleep, not to force a specific sleep time line. Artificially creating some time line that does not work for you and your twins leads to unnecessary guilt and frustration—ironically resulting in less restorative sleep for you and your babies.

Teaching healthy sleep habits prepares your children for a lifetime of restful sleep. You and your babies will be thankful you patiently took steps to ensure healthy sleep.

CHAPTER 8

Crucial
Survival
Tips

T I P #42: Make Doctor Visits Productive for You and Your Babies

A visit to the doctor can be a dreaded obligation or a welcome opportunity to discuss your twins' health.

I have been all over the place when it comes to preparing for a doctor's appointment. I have been the frazzled mother who scurries in and out of the office not remembering a thing the doctor said because I was too flustered to engage in any real conversation or to take notes. I have also been the calm, relaxed mother of twins who has figured out how to go to the doctor's office with less stress and more energy to enjoy open discussion with the doctor and to remember important things discussed.

How can you make every doctor's appointment productive instead of painful? Here are some secrets to making your doctor visits count:

- *Go to visits with a friend.* You will be much more relaxed with one adult per child. If you absolutely must go alone with both babies, ask ahead of time if the doctor's office can provide a nurse, medical assistant, volunteer, or any other health provider to assist you during the exam.
- *Consider taking one child at a time.* I found this worked well when my twins got older and more mobile. Having one child per visit helped my doctor and me stay organized and focused on the specific needs of each child.
- *Book two back-to-back appointments for your babies.* If you'd like to bring your babies together, let the appointment setter know that you have twins. With two back-to-back

TWIN HINTS
Choosing the Right Doctor for Twins

I don't think it is fair or feasible to demand that every doctor have extensive experience in caring for twins. Many excellent doctors see twins in their practice for the first time when you become their patient. The important thing is to choose a physician who has the right qualities to care for twins.

Look for a doctor who is open to questions, patient and flexible, easily accessible by phone or e-mail, and willing to spend time researching answers to questions about twins that he or she is unsure about.

I have had doctors ask me questions about twins in their practice, and I see that as a great sign of the ideal type of doctor to care for twins: they understand that caring for twins is not the same as caring for singletons, and they are willing to seek answers for their patients when needed.

appointments, you will have double the time to spend with your doctor.

+ *Make vaccinations less painful.* Give your babies a dose of Tylenol before their appointment for shots. At the doctor's office, ask if they have a numbing cream to put on your babies' thighs. When you have two babies who have to undergo shots, making vaccines less painful for them will make things less painful for everyone else, too.

+ *Ask if two nurses can give the shots, if possible.* Twins cry sympathetically. After one baby sees the other crying, you can be sure it will be much more difficult to get the other one to hold still for shots.

+ *Bring a list of questions.* A list will help you remember to discuss your most pressing concerns with your doctor.

+ *E-mail your doctor ahead of time.* If your doctor has an electronic communication system, consider e-mailing your questions ahead of time. That way, your doctor can answer some of your questions before the visit or prepare answers for discussion at the visit. You may even get the benefit of printed handouts or a list of resources if your doctor has adequate lead time.

+ *Keep a written record of key items.* It's easy to forget things unless you get them in writing. Write down your doctor's advice, answers to your questions, and any other salient points you want to remember. Take home educational handouts of interest, and ask for a printed, updated copy of your child's vaccinations. When the receptionist asks you if you want an appointment reminder card, always say yes.

- *Get a good night's sleep in preparation.* The night before your appointment, try to get some extra sleep. This will give you a rested body to tend to your babies and a rested mind to converse with your doctor.
- *See these visits as a positive experience.* Remember that you are doing something beneficial and healthy for your babies by taking them to the doctor. You want to relay this message to your babies. Babies easily pick up on their parents' emotional cues. If you are calm, relaxed, and happy, your babies will have less anxiety and even enjoy their time with their doctor. As a pediatrician, I have seen many kids, even after vaccines, smile and wave good-bye to me on their way out the door. If you and your doctor have a positive attitude about your visits, your babies will too.

TWIN HINTS
Infant Development Clinic

If you have preemie twins, ask your doctor if there is an infant development clinic in your area. Preemies have unique nutritional needs, growth patterns, and developmental time lines. They may require special testing and medical surveillance. Infant development clinics are specialty clinics designed to medically care for premature babies in conjunction with your doctor. These clinics are typically staffed by multiple health care providers, including developmental pediatricians, nutritionists, and occupational therapists. They provide routine, periodic monitoring of your preemie babies in addition to well-child and sick visits with your regular doctor. You can often find these clinics at university hospitals, children's hospitals, and other large pediatric practices.

 # #43: Get All the Help You Can

When I gave birth to Faith and Hope, I had plenty of offers of help. Initially I took on an independent spirit and wanted to do everything on my own. I even rejected my husband's offers of help at home once he went back to work.

After months of bed rest and having to depend on others, I felt liberated and independent. I wanted to be Supermom. I tried to take care of Faith and Hope all by myself. I even stayed up all night by myself pumping breast milk, feeding the babies, and changing them.

That lasted about all of four weeks. After a month, my friend, the babies' pediatrician, said to me, "You really look tired." An understated person, what she meant was, "You look like hell!"

Her words and several horrible bouts of mastitis (a painful inflammation of the breasts) brought me back to my senses. As soon as I asked for aid, the help came pouring in. My family took turns helping to feed, diaper, and dress our twins. My husband, Chris, and I shared night duties, with breaks provided by family volunteers. By the time I revisited our pediatrician, she said, "You look like yourself again." I have concealer, blush, and my wonderful family to thank for that response!

My advice to mothers of multiples is to take all the help you can get! Take any help from people you trust. Don't be a martyr. If you don't want someone to care for the babies, ask for help around the house with cooking or cleaning. Caring for multiples

---

TWIN HINTS
Mommy's Helpers

If you don't have an extensive network of friends or relatives where you live, you can often find inexpensive "mommy's helpers" (certified teenage babysitters) in your neighborhood.

If you don't feel comfortable with your helper directly caring for your babies, you can still use this person to help you hold the babies, play with them, or assist with household duties. Mommy's helpers are also great for keeping older siblings entertained while you tend to your newborn twins.

Twin Story
Teamwork at Its Best

Dr. Kimberly Douglas, mother to twin girls, relates this story about the importance of family and friends in caring for twin babies:

After giving birth, I was readmitted to the intensive care unit for hypertension. My poor husband, Steve! While I had around-the-clock care in the hospital, he had three children to care for. By all accounts, he did very well, but I could just imagine him with a three-year-old and two newborns.

For this, we called in all the offers of help, and they all came in! Neighbors were there day and night, so Steve could come visit me as well as get some sleep. Family starting flying in from all coasts.

After I came home and Steve went back to work, we were so lucky that my in-laws were retired. Being the parents of twins themselves, they were very supportive! At night, Steve's mom and dad would take one shift, followed by his sister, followed by myself. During the day, we took turns taking naps.

After Steve's sister went back to work, Steve's parents took longer shifts until 2:00 A.M. and I was on from 2:00 A.M. until the morning. I was very thankful for them and sad when they flew back to Canada after two months.

It basically comes down to having fantastic support. We consider ourselves very lucky for all the help we received.

is a full-time job, so let others help you. Let them give you a break, even if it's only for an hour or two between feedings.

My family's motto is, "It takes a village." We know that caring for a child is much easier when everyone close to that child participates in raising him or her.

If you have a group of friends or relatives who are willing to be your "village," I encourage you to let them in. You will find that not only will you be happier, but your children will thrive on the extra attention.

TIP #44: Don't Let Crying Stress You Out

Every mother of twins faces days when she cannot appease two babies at once, no matter how hard she tries. You have fed them, changed them, and checked to make sure they are not sick. When you calm one baby down, the other baby screams. Despite your efforts, you get crying in succession or, better yet, in crystal-clear stereo.

As your babies cry, your body begins to tense. You feel stressed. You start to think that you're a terrible mother. What is happening here?

Why do we feel so horrible when our babies cry? The answer lies in our body's built-in programming. Nature designed parents to respond (and to respond quickly!) to a child's cry. When we hear our babies cry, our bodies release stress hormones, most notably adrenaline. With increasing adrenaline, our hearts race, our blood pressure climbs, and a pressing need to appease the crying child switches on. When the crying continues, your brain hears the message: "You're a terrible mother. You're neglecting your babies. Tend to them fast!" This vital instinct was designed to protect babies by preventing them from being abandoned and neglected.

The problem is that this primal instinct cannot distinguish the difference between an attentive mother and a negligent mother. And it doesn't cut you any slack because you have twins. As long as your babies cry, your body will respond by making you feel anxious and stressed until the crying stops.

During these trying times, it's important to maintain your cool and reduce your body's stress level so that you can care for your babies calmly and lovingly. The next time crying has your pulse rising, consider the following stress-relieving techniques:

- *Breathe deeply.* Take a few long, deep breaths. This reduces your heart rate and helps to relieve pent-up tension.
- *Use positive self-talk.* Remind yourself of how much you love your babies and that you're not a bad mother just because your twins are crying. The fact is that sometimes babies cry no matter what you do. Experts believe that some babies cry simply to let off steam. Your job is to be there for your babies, to make sure that they aren't sick and that their needs are met, and to show them that you love them even when they cry. If you're doing these things, you're doing a great job!
- *Look toward the future with optimism.* Babies of loving, attentive mothers ultimately cry less as they mature. You and your babies have a bright future ahead of you!

+ *Take a short break.* If you start to feel on edge and your stress level becomes overwhelming, it's time to give yourself a short break. Kiss your babies, tell them that you love them, and then put them down in a safe place like their crib while you leave the room for a few minutes. Distancing yourself from the sound of crying will naturally lower the adrenaline in your system, restore your mental and emotional state, and allow you to attend to your babies in a more relaxed state.
+ *Ask for help.* If it takes you longer than a few minutes to recuperate, call your partner or friend to help watch your twins while you regain your composure. A short walk, shower, or nap can offer emotionally restorative benefits.
+ *Cry if you need to.* During your break, it is totally acceptable and even healthy to cry if you want to. Crying releases pent-up tension and serves to lower your stress level. As one wise mother of twins put it, "Sometimes an indulgent cry does wonders."

The next time crying has you stressed out, remember that crying is simply a form of communication for our babies. They are telling us that they need and want us. Our body's response to our babies' crying not only reminds us of our obligation to attend to their needs but also speaks of the special, magnetic bond that we share with them as parent and children.

#45: Aim for Fairness, Not Equality

Angela and Amy are fraternal twin sisters. At their fourth birthday party, their mother bought festive birthday balloons inscribed with their names. As the colorful balloons floated merrily announcing "Happy Birthday Angela!" and "Happy Birthday Amy!" Amy cried hysterically in her aunt's arms. Why? Her balloons had fewer letters than her sister's balloons and that wasn't fair!

Or was it fair but not equal? Children often equate fairness with equality, and one of the most important lessons to teach our children (and remind ourselves) is that fairness and equality are not always synonymous.

Equality in parenting means treating our children the same. Fairness means treating them justly and with their individual differences and circumstances in mind.

As a parent of twins, I completely understand how the two terms can become so easily confused when rearing twins. Parents of singletons have fewer issues with treating each child differently because the age difference provides a natural, built-in system of individualization. For example, Sammy gets presents today while you don't because it's his birthday and not yours. With a pair of young twins, this age stratification doesn't exist, resulting in more confusion both for parents and twin children.

When I first brought Faith and Hope home from the hospital, I was determined to treat them exactly the same. If I held one baby for five minutes, I made sure I held the other baby for exactly five minutes. I dressed them alike, offered them the exact same amount of formula, and alternated who was first to be fed.

Like many other well-meaning novice parents of twins, I tried to do everything the same because I wanted to make sure that one child did not get preferential treatment. I was afraid that treating one differently would produce one well-adjusted and one maladjusted child. To ensure that each baby had an equal chance at succeeding in life, I felt I had to make things perfectly equal.

Faith and Hope taught me very quickly that they were individuals with differences, even as babies. For example, Faith initially had more gastrointestinal problems and needed to be held more often, while Hope was able to contently interact with me from her bouncy chair. If I forced equal arm time with Hope, Faith would cry and upset Hope, resulting in two crying babies. The following month, their needs completely reversed. Through instances like these, I learned that I had to give up my strict adherence to everything being equal and instead embrace the joy of doing what was right for each baby.

It's important to teach our twins this important difference as they mature. By instructing them that fairness is not always the same as equality, they learn important lifelong lessons:

+ It will encourage them to explore and rejoice in their individuality. "Mommy and Daddy do not treat me exactly the same as my sister because I'm a unique and different person."
+ By showing them that treatment that is right for one person is not always right for another, we teach them perspective-taking, empathy, and social tolerance. "Mommy has to hold Faith more right now because Faith is sick and I'm not."

TWIN HINTS
Easy Ways to Teach the Difference
Between Fairness and Equality

+ Reward positive behavior. By learning that positive behaviors result in differential treatment, your twins are more likely to understand why negative behaviors are also to be treated differentially.
+ Encourage individuality. Knowing that people are unique builds tolerance for differential treatment based on individual needs.
+ Encourage sharing. Having a generous spirit will reduce their desire to have everything equal.
+ Model fairness by catering to individual needs and not wants.
+ Give your children choices. Learning that there are choices in life will build their understanding of why you may choose to treat each child differently.
+ When disciplining a child, consider giving him or her two options. Since your child made the choice, he or she will be more likely to feel the treatment is fair.
+ When your child says something is not fair, explain why you are treating your children differentially. It may not immediately satisfy him or her, but over time, your children will grasp the concept that there is a reason for your actions.
+ When your twins become old enough, let them work out some of their conflicts over fairness on their own.

- It will teach them that positive actions and attitudes often result in preferential positive treatment—fair but unequal treatment. "I get to play with Legos an extra fifteen minutes while Billy goes to bed because I did my homework quietly while Billy threw a tantrum over doing his."

The next time you feel that twinge of parental guilt because you think you aren't treating your twins the same or you hear that oh-so-familiar outcry, "It's not fair!" remember that fairness and equality are not always synonymous—and they shouldn't be. We are doing our children a lifelong favor by teaching them early how to differentiate between the two.

T I P #46: Make Time for Talk

Talk with your twins as much as you can. Time with an engaged and conversing adult can have a profound impact on a child's development.

The Research
The influence of parent-child conversation on a child's language abilities was first documented comprehensively in a landmark study by Dr. Betty Hart and Dr. Todd Risley in their 1995 book, *Meaningful Differences in the Everyday Lives of Young American Children*. After following forty-two families and analyzing over thirteen hundred hours of adult-child conversation, they found that the more adult words children heard during their first three years of life, the greater their language, IQ, and academic potential.

More recently, Dr. Jill Gilkerson and her research team at Infoture, a Colorado-based company, confirmed the impact of parent conversation on a child's language development. Dr. Gilkerson used a digital language processor and language analysis software to record and analyze over eighteen thousand hours of conversation in more than three hundred American homes. In their study, children who heard more adult words per day scored better on standardized language assessment tests than children exposed to fewer words.

The message from these studies is clear: the more adult talk children hear, the greater their potential for language development.

TWIN HINTS
LENA (Language ENvironment Analysis)

If you want an objective measure of your child's language exposure, Infoture sells to families the same digital language processor it uses for its language research. This two-ounce device, called LENA, uses revolutionary technology to measure and analyze a child's language environment. Children wear the device in the front pocket of special clothing designed for maximal audio capture. At the end of the day, you can see the number of adult words your child heard throughout the day. This is a powerful tool for motivating parental speech on a daily basis. It's also a fantastic way to measure the amount of language your child is exposed to while under the care of a nanny or other child care provider. You can purchase LENA directly from Infoture online at www.lenababy.com.

Why This Research Matters to Twins

Twins have a greater risk for language delays than singletons for several reasons. The most significant include decreased parental attention and considerable parental fatigue due to the physical demands of caring for twins. These social factors can limit twins' exposure to engaging adult interaction and conversation.

But there is good news! Experts agree that the language delay seen in twins is largely environmental. In other words, there is something we can do about it. You have the power to maximize your twins' language potential. The more adult speech you can expose your children to, the better. And the sooner, the better.

It's easier than it may at first seem to build language-rich activities into your everyday life. Here are some simple talking tips for fellow busy parents:

- *Talk to your twins during normal, everyday activities.* Meals present a wonderful opportunity to talk about the color, taste, and texture of foods. Baths are great for naming body parts.
- *Think out loud.* Whether it's your grocery list or ideas for your upcoming sales pitch, speak these things out loud to your children.
- *Talk to them during play.* Describe what you are doing. Describe what they are doing. Name their toys, and join in their creative fantasies.
- *Read to them.* It doesn't even have to be kids' books all the time. You can read newspapers, magazines, or your favorite book (*Moby Dick* anyone?).

TWIN FACTS *Do Twins Create Their Own Language?*

Do twins really have an exclusive and secret language? Myths aside, here are the facts:

- The development of a true "private language" is relatively uncommon. One study reported a rate of 12 percent in twin toddlers and 6 percent in three-year-old twins.
- Private language is more common in boys and identical twins.
- Private language can be associated with poor developmental outcomes.
- The majority of what is thought to be a private language is in fact normal toddler speech—young twins speaking a culturally appropriate language but in an immature manner. Twin toddlers understand each other when adults don't due to shared social context. This more common type of "twin talk" has been appropriately termed "shared understanding."
- An estimated 50 percent of twin toddlers demonstrate shared understanding.
- Both types of twin talk decrease over time.

* *Sing to them.* Belt out your favorite kids' songs, rock and roll, even made-up songs! Be creative and have fun!
* *Give them one-on-one time.* Make sure each twin has individual play time with each parent. These bonding moments help build your children's speech and language abilities.
* *Invite your friends and family over.* Having more adults around can increase each twin's one-on-one time with an adult and their overall adult speech exposure.

Begin today to talk to your twins as much as possible. Talk about everything you can. Talk to them even though they don't talk back. Babies begin acquiring language skills long before they utter their first recognizable word. The first years of a child's life represent a critical time of brain and language development. Although it may seem silly to speak to a baby who doesn't appear to speak back, know that your children are indeed listening—and learning!

T I P #47: Make Time for Play

My mother always says, "A child's job is to eat, sleep, and play. If they aren't doing one of those things, then something is wrong." My wise mother could not be more right. As someone who trains future pediatricians, I teach my residents to look for deficiencies in those three things as a possible sign of illness, neglect, or developmental delay.

Children need to play just as much as they need to eat and sleep! Play and exploration during play develop a child's motor abilities as well as cognitive abilities (intellect). Allow your twins to play with each other, and make time for them to play with you, too.

Twin Play

Twins have the obvious social advantage of having an immediate
and readily available playmate. They can provide a ready source of
visual, auditory, and social stimulation for each other.

To maximize your twins' play time together, I recommend
the following:

- Have enough toys around so they aren't constantly fighting
  for the same toy. But you don't have to buy two of everything.
  You'll want them to learn early on the importance of sharing.
- Have a variety of toys so they can explore.
- Encourage interaction between them. Faith and Hope loved
  building towers together with plastic interlocking bricks.
- For older toddlers, have plenty of dress-up items, dolls,
  puppets, and other toys that stimulate cooperative and
  pretend play.
- Buy a ball. See the Twin Hints box in this section.
- Take your children outside as much as possible—in your
  own yard or to a nearby playground. There are so many
  stimulating things to do outdoors under age-appropriate,
  careful supervision.
- Keep a watchful eye on your twins. Toys can easily become
  weapons when you have two babies. Also, two active, curious twin toddlers have an uncanny way of using their dual
  brains and strength to create unsafe "games" for themselves.
- Take lots of pictures! There is nothing like seeing a pair of
  twins generously share toys or make each other laugh during
  play. These precious moments melt your heart and remind
  you of how blessed you really are to have twins.

Play Time with Mommy and Daddy

Twins are truly fortunate to have each other as ready playmates. Their time together affords them many social, emotional, and physical benefits. But twins also need time with you. Experts agree that twins need to bond with, learn from, and spend quality time with adults in order to maximize their developmental potential.

You are immensely vital to your child's development. A co-twin cannot replace the role of parent interaction and play, and neither can the most expensive educational toys, videos, or computer programs. You are the single most well-designed toy for your child. No toy can ever impart the variety of intellectual, social, and physical stimulation that you can provide. The best

---

TWIN HINTS
Buy a Ball

Balls are one of my favorite developmental toys for twins. When Faith and Hope were around nine months old, I would roll a ball, and they would race to get it. This friendly competition resulted in the rapid development of their crawling ability. Now that they are toddlers, I sit with them, and we roll the ball to each other. This engaging activity teaches them the important social skill of taking turns. My husband, Chris, likes to juggle balls or spin them on his finger. My children watch with delight as they learn about object motion and gravity (yes, every circus act has to end somehow). In the near future, I foresee us playing handball or four-square to practice the concept of rules in play. The possibilities are endless!

TWIN HINTS	
Top Ten Favorite Toys for Infants	

1. Hanging mobile	Birth+
2. Baby mirror (for example, Fisher-Price Ocean Wonders Musical Activity Mirror, Lamaze First Mirror)	Birth+
3. Play gym (for example, Fisher-Price Melodies and Lights Deluxe Gym)	Birth+
4. Baby rattles and teething rings	4 months+
5. Bouncy chair with swivel seat and activity center	6 months+
6. Ball (should be much larger than an infant's mouth)	6 months+
7. Large piano-type keyboard (for example, Little Tikes Baby Tap-a-Tune Piano)	9 months+
8. Stackable rings (for example, Fisher-Price Dance Baby Dance! Classical Stacker)	9 months+
9. Simple shape sorters (for example, Fisher-Price Peek-a-Blocks shape sorter)	9 months+
10. Books (I like soft, cloth ones for young infants)	All ages

thing is that you are priceless, and yet you are free to your child. Give to your child the gift of play with you today.

Here are some easy ways you can actively engage your twins in play:

- Talk to them during play.
- Describe what you are doing.
- Describe what they are doing.
- Show them how a toy works.
- Make one parent the "play parent" and the other the "duty parent" for a few hours, and then switch roles.
- Make routine time also play time. For example, baths can be a lot of fun with bubbles, toys, and lots of splashing.
- Be silly and have fun! Having children is your excuse to be a kid again.

T I P #48: Don't Forget the Older Siblings

Siblings deserve special consideration. It's not unusual for the squeaky wheel to get the grease, and twins are squeaky!

Siblings need preparation for the birth of twins. They also require special and solo attention after the twins come home. With thoughtful planning and continued surveillance, you can ensure that siblings not only accept the addition of twins to the family but also fully welcome them. After all, they have just inherited two new playmates!

Here are some ways to keep siblings happy and engaged:

- Show them ultrasound pictures of the babies.
- Tell them that two babies will be coming home.
- I love the book *The New Baby* by Mercer Mayer to prepare children for the arrival of newborn siblings.
- If the twins require hospitalization, I recommend bringing siblings into the NICU to visit.
- Buy siblings homecoming presents "from the twins."
- Be patient if older siblings initially show some signs of jealousy. Acknowledge how they feel, and reaffirm your love for them.
- If they seem interested, allow older siblings to help care for the babies. This helps them feel proud and nurturing in their role as older siblings.
- Let siblings acclimate to having the twins at home before requiring them do any chores related to the twins.
- Include the older children in pictures with the twins.
- Plan one-on-one time with the older siblings. You can take older siblings out on a day trip alone with you.
- Parents can take turns caring for the babies to allow each parent exclusive time with the older children.
- Shower plenty of affection on siblings.
- Show siblings how they can play with the babies. Tell them how lucky they are to have two instant, lifelong friends and playmates. Let them know how lucky the twins are to have them as older siblings.
- Let older siblings go to bed a little later than your twins so they can have one-on-one time with you.

- Continue to encourage family time. Select an activity you all enjoy. Reading books out loud every night is a great way to get everyone involved in one activity.
- Model positive behavior. The happier, more relaxed, and overtly thankful you are about the twins, the more likely your other children will be too. Smile, laugh, and enjoy each day! If you do, your children will too.

TIP #49: Make Time for Yourselves

Every parent should try to spend small increments of time alone, away from child-rearing duties. For most parents of twins, short breaks for each parent can easily be achieved by babysitting for each other.

The greater challenge for many parents of multiples is spending quality time together as a couple. Parents of twins know how much work it requires to care for twins. Because of this, they hesitate to leave their babies in the care of others unless absolutely necessary.

I consider time together away from your twins a true necessity. Every couple should make it a priority to carve out some time together.

Short breaks for dinner or a movie can revive your energy, allowing you to better care for your babies. A strong relationship between parents trickles down to better teamwork in accomplishing the daily duties of parenthood. A happy and cohesive partnership models healthy interactions for your twins. When parents make time to renew their energy and strengthen their relationship, the whole family benefits.

These are some of my favorite stress-relieving, partnership-bonding activities for parents:

+ Go on a short walk together. Hold hands as you stroll.
+ Go to the movies together. Treat yourselves to popcorn, candy, soda, and all the other junk food you don't want your kids to see you eat.
+ Make a reservation for two at your favorite restaurant.
+ Rent a tandem bike at the beach or park and ride it together.
+ If there is a lake nearby, go canoeing or kayaking. Rowing requires teamwork. Plus, it can be very calming to be surrounded by the serenity of water.
+ Jointly engage in an artistic activity. Paint together. Sing together. Write a poem together.
+ Get uninterrupted sleep together. My husband and I always joke about this, but it's true: we go on annual weekend trips to Las Vegas, Nevada . . . to sleep!
+ Go to a place that you went to when you were dating. Plan a romantic evening together. Tell each other again all the things that made you fall in love.

Be creative and pursue whatever activity you enjoy together. Whatever you do, relax, get rest, and remember how fortunate you are to have each other and the lovely children you have waiting for you at home.

#50: Share Your Experience with Novice Mothers of Twins

Caring for twins is like being in labor: anyone who says it isn't painful is lying. Yet at the same time, it is beautiful and miraculous. In the end, you are thankful for having gone through it. You feel proud of what you have achieved. And there is the lovely amnesia of the pain—not that you forget that it hurt but you forget just how much. Just enough amnesia that you would even go through it all again.

No one can really convey the intense pain and joy of labor. The same is true with parenting twins. However, only those who have lived through the experience can begin to understand and describe it.

You have wisdom and insight that only a parent of twins can provide. Your knowledge can make a major difference in the lives of other parents. I encourage you at every stage in your parenting journey to share your experience and advice with novice mothers of twins. By teaching others, you can appreciate your own accomplishments while helping others to achieve parenting success.

TWIN HINTS
Sharing What You Know

You can make a major difference in the lives of other mothers by sharing your stories and advice for parenting twins. Below are some easy ways to get started:

- Join a local Mothers of Twins group.
- Visit online forums for parents of multiples. Answer questions that others post.
- Feel free to submit your tips and ideas for online posting at my twins' health Web site: www.twinsdoctor.com.
- Start you own online blog about life with twins.
- Attend some local and national twin events.
- Gather some local twin mothers and start your own twins club.
- Chat with other mothers of multiples wherever you go. By simply greeting them as a fellow mother of twins, you open up doors for an enriching exchange of ideas and experiences. To this day, I continue to learn so much about mothering twins through these delightful chance encounters.

Whether being a twin or being a parent to twins, having twins in your life is a true blessing. Enjoy these final inspiring quotes:

It was great growing up as a twin. We really valued our individuality, but to this day, we are the closest of friends and more like-minded than any of our other friends.

—Angela Sun, twin sister to Amy Sun

The bottom line is that twins are hard work. There is no easy way out of it. But in the end, what you realize is that twins really do have a special bond, whether they're identical or fraternal. It's in the way they develop and grow together. They could be 180 degrees different in personality, but still love and rely on each other.

—Anh Tran, mother to twin boys

RESOURCES

Twin Pregnancy Books

Everything You Need to Know to Have a Healthy Twin Pregnancy,
Gila Leiter and Rachel Kranz (Dell, 2000).

*Expecting Twins, Triplets, and More: A Doctor's Guide to a Healthy
and Happy Multiple Pregnancy,* Rachel Franklin (St. Martin's
Griffin, 2005).

*The Multiple Pregnancy Sourcebook: Pregnancy and the First Days
with Twins, Triplets, and More,* Nancy Bowers (McGraw-
Hill, 2001).

*When You're Expecting Twins, Triplets, or Quads, Revised Edition:
Proven Guidelines for a Healthy Multiple Pregnancy,* Barbara
Luke and Tamara Eberlein (HarperCollins, 2004).

Your Pregnancy Quick Guide: Twins, Triplets, and More, Glade B.
Curtis and Judith Schuler (Da Capo Lifelong Books, 2005).

Twin Parenting Books Authored by Physicians

Twins! 2e: Pregnancy, Birth and the First Year of Life, Connie
Agnew, Alan Klein, and Jill Ganon (HarperCollins, 2006).

*Twins and Multiple Births: The Essential Parenting Handbook from
Pregnancy to Adulthood,* Carol Cooper (Random House,
2004).

Twin Parenting Books Focused on the Early Years

The Everything Twins, Triplets, and More Book: From Seeing the First Sonogram to Coordinating Nap Times and Feedings— All You Need to Enjoy Your Multiples, Pamela Fierro (Adams Media Corporation, 2005).

Having Twins and More: A Parent's Guide to Multiple Pregnancy, Birth, and Early Childhood, Elizabeth Noble (Houghton Mifflin, 2003).

Mothering Multiples: Breastfeeding and Caring for Twins or More! Karen Kerkoff Gramada (La Leche International, 2007).

Raising Twins: What Parents Want to Know (and What Twins Want to Tell Them), Eileen Pearlman and Jill Ganon (HarperCollins, 2000).

Ready or Not, Here We Come! The Real Experts' Guide to the First Year with Twins, Elizabeth Lyons (Finn-Phyllis Press, 2007).

Twins: A Practical Guide to Parenting Multiples from Conception to Preschool, Katrina Bowman and Louise Ryan (Allen & Unwin, 2005).

Twinspiration: Real-Life Advice from Pregnancy Through the First Year, Cheryl Lage (Taylor Trade Publishing, 2006).

Twin Parenting Books with Information for Older Twins

Emotionally Healthy Twins: A New Philosophy for Parenting Two Unique Children, Joan Friedman (Da Capo Lifelong Books, 2008).

It's Twins! Parent-to-Parent Advice from Infancy Through Adolescence, Susan Heim (Hampton Roads Publishing Company, 2007).

Raising Twins After the First Year: Everything You Need to Know About Bringing Up Twins—From Toddlers to Preteens, Karen Gottesman (Marlowe & Company, 2006).

Ready or Not, There We Go! The Real Experts' Guide to the Toddler Years with Twins, Elizabeth Lyons (Finn-Phyllis Press, 2006).

Recommended General Parenting Books

Boys and Girls Learn Differently! A Guide for Teachers and Parents, Michael Gurian (Jossey-Bass, 2002).

Caring for Your Baby and Young Child: Birth to Age Five, Steven P. Shelov, ed. (Bantam, 2004).

Don't Give Me That Attitude! Twenty-Four Rude, Selfish, Insensitive Things Kids Do and How to Stop Them, Michele Borba (Jossey-Bass, 2004).

From First Kicks to First Steps, Alan Greene (McGraw-Hill, 2004).

Nurture the Nature: Understanding and Supporting Your Child's Unique Core Personality, Michael Gurian (Jossey-Bass, 2007).

Raising Baby Green: The Earth-Friendly Guide to Pregnancy, Childbirth, and Baby Care, Alan Greene (Jossey-Bass, 2007).

Twelve Simple Secrets Real Moms Know: Getting Back to Basics and Raising Happy Kids, Michele Borba (Jossey-Bass, 2006).

Twin Books for Twin Children

Just Like Me, Barbara Neasi (Children's Press, 2003).

Little Miss Twins, Robert Hargreaves (Price Stern Sloan, 2000).

Princess Poppy: The Baby Twins, Janey Louise Jones (Corgi, 2008).

Twins Go to Bed, Ellen Weiss (Aladdin, 2004).

Twins in the Park, Ellen Weiss (Aladdin, 2003).
Twins Take a Bath, Ellen Weiss (Aladdin, 2003).
Twin to Twin, Margaret O'Hair (Margaret K. McElderry, 2003).
Two Times the Fun, Beverly Cleary (HarperCollins, 2005).

Twin Parenting Magazines

Multiples Magazine, www.multiplesmag.com. A newly established
    magazine for parents of multiples. The first edition was
    released in December 2007.
TWINS Magazine, www.twinsmagazine.com. Established in
    1984, this was the first magazine exclusively about twins.

General Parenting Magazines

American Baby, www.americanbaby.com. Focused on expectant
    and new mothers.
Cookie Magazine, www.cookiemag.com. Hip and stylish. *Cookie*
    "believes that being a good parent and maintaining your
    sense of style are not mutually exclusive."
Parenting Magazine, www.parenting.com. *Parenting* targets a broad
    audience and boasts a circulation rate of over two million.
Parents Magazine, www.parents.com. The oldest parenting
    magazine and a household staple for young families.

National and International Support Organizations

Australian Multiple Births Association, www.amba.org.au. The
    Australian national organization for multiples.
Multiple Births Canada, www.multiplebirthscanada.org. The
    Canadian national organization for multiples.

National Organization of Mother of Twins Clubs, www.nomotc
.org. A U.S. national organization for multiples with over
25,000 members and 475 local clubs.

TAMBA, www.tamba.org.uk. The United Kingdom national
organization for multiples.

Organizations Dedicated to Twin Research
Center for the Study of Multiple Birth, www.multiplebirth.com.
Twins Foundation, www.twinsfoundation.com.

Twin Pregnancy Web Sites
Marvelous Multiples, www.marvelousmultiples.com. Offers
information on maintaining a healthy twin pregnancy.

Sidelines, www.sidelines.org. Supports mothers with high-risk
pregnancies, especially those requiring bed rest.

TTTS Foundation, www.tttsfoundation.org. Organization
dedicated to twin pregnancies complicated by twin-to-twin
transfusion syndrome.

Twin Parenting and Health Web Sites
About.com, Twins and Multiples, www.multiples.about.com.

Talk About Twins, www.talk-about-twins.com.

Twin Advice, www.twinadvice.com.

TwinsDoctor.com, www.twinsdoctor.com.

Twinsinfo.com, www.twinsinfo.com.

Twins List, www.twinslist.org.

Twin Online Forums

Twinshock, www.twinshock.net.
Twinstuff Community, www.twinstuff.com.

Twin Internet Stores

The Best Dressed Child, www.bestdressedchild.com.
Double Blessings, www.doubleblessings.com.
Double Up Books, www.doubleupbooks.com.
Ever So Tiny, www.eversotiny.ca.
Just 4 Twins, www.just4twins.com.
Just Multiples, www.justmultiples.com.
Nurture Place, www.nurtureplace.com.
The Preemie Store, www.preemiestore.com.
Twinshoppe, www.twinshoppe.com.
Twinstuff Store, www.twinstuff.com/store/catalog.
Twinz Gear, www.twinzgear.com.

Twin DNA Testing

Affiliated Genetics, www.affiliatedgenetics.com. Founded by
    an obstetrician with specialized training in maternal-
    fetal medicine and genetics. Accredited by the American
    Association of Blood Banks.
DNA Solutions, www.dnanow.com. Offers low-cost DNA
    testing. Member of the International Standardization
    Organization.

Twin TV Shows and Documentaries for Parents

In the Womb—Multiples (National Geographic, 2007). Amazing look at multiples as they develop and interact inside the womb. Originally aired on the National Geographic Channel. Available on DVD.

Jon and Kate Plus 8 (Discovery Health Channel and TLC, first aired in 2007). Reality show featuring a family with a pair of twins and a set of sextuplets.

The Twin Connection (A&E, 2006). Explores the powerful and mysterious bond between twins. Available on DVD.

Your Babies' Journey—Twins, Triplets and Quads (Pioneer Productions, 2006). DVD produced by a company specializing in science documentaries. Navigation menus allow parents to view various stages of fetal development corresponding to their particular stage of pregnancy.

G-Rated Films and Videos for Children with Twin Main Characters

These are not intended for children under two years of age.

Billboard Dad (1998).
Escape to Witch Mountain (1975).
Getting There (2002).
To Grandmother's House We Go (1992).
How the West Was Fun (1994).
The Little Twins: Tales of Enchantment (1998).
The Little Twins: The Magic of Giving (1998).
Our Lips Are Sealed (1995).
The Parent Trap (1961).

Passport to Paris (1999).
The Prince and the Pauper (1937).
Return to Witch Mountain (1978).
Rolie Polie Olie: Baby Bot Chase (2003).
Rugrats: Phil and Lil Double Trouble (1991).
The Suite Life of Zack and Cody: Sweet Suite Victory (2005).
The Suite Life of Zack and Cody: Taking Over the Tipton (2005).
Switching Goals (1999).
When in Rome (2002).
Winning London (2001).

Twin Talent Agencies
Twins Talent, www.twinstalent.tv. The only talent agency
dedicated solely to twins.

Annual Twin Conferences and Events
Australian Multiple Births Association Annual Conference,
www.amba.org.au.
France Twins Day, a.loyer.chez-alice.fr. Annual twins gathering
every August 15 in Pleaucadeuc, France. Great excuse to
travel to France!
The International Twins Association, www.intltwins.org. Hosts
social events for twins.
Multiple Births Canada Annual Conference, www.multiple
birthscanada.org.
National Organization of Mothers of Twins Club Annual
Conference, www.nomotc.org.

Twins World, www.twinsworld.com. Keeps an updated list of
  twin events around the world.
Twinsburg Annual Twins Day Festival, www.twinsdays.org.
  This annual festival held in Twinsburg, Ohio, had over two
  thousand sets of twins in 2007.

ABOUT THE AUTHOR

Khanh-Van Le-Bucklin, M.D., M.O.M., is an academic pediatrician with over fifteen years of experience in health education. She currently directs multiple aspects of education at the University of California, Irvine, where she serves as pediatric residency director, pediatric electives director, and pediatric continuing medical education director. She has received multiple teaching awards for her work in medical education and has published several articles in medical journals.

Dr. Le-Bucklin has been the senior medical content editor for the pediatric Web site DrGreene.com since 1999. She is the founder of TwinsDoctor.com, a Web site with health information exclusively for multiples.

She received her undergraduate degree in integrative biology with a minor in American literature at the University of California, Berkeley. She earned her medical degree from the University of California, San Francisco, and completed her pediatric residency at Stanford University. She is a fellow of the American Academy of Pediatrics and a member of the Association of Pediatric Program Directors.

She earned her Mother of Multiples (M.O.M.) degree in 2006 with the birth of her twin daughters, Faith and Hope.

INDEX

CPSIA information can be obtained at www.ICGtesting.com
Printed in the USA
BVOW02n1357190216

437156BV00016B/24/P